People, Psychology
& Business

People, Psychology & Business

Lita de Alberdi, CPsychol

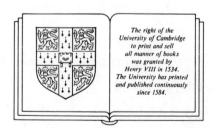

The right of the
University of Cambridge
to print and sell
all manner of books
was granted by
Henry VIII in 1534.
The University has printed
and published continuously
since 1584.

Cambridge University Press
Cambridge
New York   Port Chester   Melbourne   Sydney

To my father Ron Pearson, with love

Published by the Press Syndicate of the University of Cambridge
The Pitt Building, Trumpington Street, Cambridge CB2 1RP
40 West 20th Street, New York, NY 10011, USA
10 Stamford Road, Oakleigh, Melbourne 3166, Australia

First published 1990

Printed in Great Britain at the University Press, Cambridge

British Library cataloguing in publication data
De Alberdi, Lita, *1953-*
  People, psychology and business.
  1. Management, Psychosocial aspects
  I. Title
  658'.001'9

Library of Congress catalogue card number: 90-31055

ISBN 0 521 37618 1

GO

The author and publisher are grateful to the following
for permission to reproduce illustrations and extracts:
pp16, 17 Croom Helm Ltd; p42 M. Tysoe, Collins;
fig 7, p70 CBS Japan Ltd; pp94, 95 Hutchinson, London

contents

5. *intragroup dynamics* 68

6. *group work* 83

preface

As human beings, the single most important thing in our environment is other people. Other people constitute our social environment, a reality created and sustained by people. We can call it *social reality* to distinguish it from the rest of our environment.

Work – involvement in work, success at work – creates another special kind of social reality, one in which the rules of interpersonal relationships are more circumscribed and constrained, governed as it is by an explicit role structure (manager, secretary, receptionist, programmer). For at least eight hours of our waking day most of us are involved in the social reality of work.

This involvement forces us to adapt, compromise and restrain our behaviour towards the people with whom we work. Because of the explicitly formalised nature of the social reality of work, behaviour is, to some extent, predictable, in the sense that work roles contain detailed descriptions of the types of activities required for satisfactory performance of the job. Comparisons can be made between the job description and the actual performance of the job-holder. However, people are still people and thus prone to all the biases they have always been prone to. Social process still finds a way to operate within and between these formalised/regularised role structures.

You may be a manager but you are also a person, as is everyone around you. You could say that inside the role is a person looking out. Goffman described us as wearing masks (roles) and being actors on a stage (as in Shakespeare's 'All the world's a stage and all the men and women merely players').

To some extent we derive our sense of self, of identity, by interpreting the reactions of other people to our own behaviour, so they act as a sort of mirror into which we peer in order to construct our social identity. One of the most disturbing aspects of psychotics is their lack of interest in the thoughts and feelings of other people. On the other hand, some people take a great deal of account of the behaviour and reactions of other people.

However, some people misread the reactions of others and thus amend their behaviour inappropriately; some may or may not read others correctly , but they do not adjust their behaviour; some both read the situation correctly and adjust their behaviour appropriately.

When Gorbachov visited Britain in April 1989, Neil Kinnock, the leader of the Opposition at that time, remarked that Gorbachov was basically such a nice man you could not fail to get on with him. Similar comments were made by the Prime Minister Margaret Thatcher. There are many well-known people whom psychologists would describe as being 'socially skilled'. Such people use many of the 'tricks' that are described in this book for facilitating communication. There is nothing 'cynical' about doing this; it is the oil that frees interaction and allows good communication which is so essential in everyday life.

Psychology is concerned with the understanding of behaviour. To some extent we are all amateur psychologists; we watch ourselves and each other, trying to understand why people behave in the way they do. Since the vast majority of us are surrounded by people throughout our lives, it is not surprising that they are probably the single most important factor in our environment.

The study of psychology comes from philosophy. *Psyche* is the Greek word for spirit, soul or mind, *ology* means study; so *psychology* originally meant the study of the mind.

Organisations are made up of people. One important factor that contributes to success in business and industry is the ability both to understand what other people are telling us and to communicate clearly what we are trying to convey to others.

Unfortunately we are only human, and the consequence of this is that we are prone to biases and misjudgements. Many of these can be overcome if we understand *what they are* and *how they operate*. This is what this book is really about – the human side of business.

Chapters 1 and 2 are specifically concerned with interpersonal, face-to-face, one-to-one encounters. Once you understand the principles outlined you should find that you can both read behaviour correctly and also adopt the appropriate behaviour for making a favourable or desired impression upon others. Chapter 3 concentrates on motivation – how to recognise it in others, how to motivate others, and how to motivate yourself. Chapter 4 analyses leadership. Chapter 5 moves to the group level and looks at how being in a group can affect your behaviour. Chapter 6 discusses some group situations and how to handle them, and chapter 7 is about how groups relate to one another. Chapter 8 moves back to the interpersonal level with a discussion on interviewing, and finally, chapter 9 talks about a special case – technological communication and how it can be useful to you.

There are several excellent books on public speaking, giving presentations, effective report writing, and so on; these topics will not be covered here. The aim of this book is to help the student to develop effective techniques for dealing with people successfully in a variety of situations both at interpersonal (one-to-one), intergroup (group-to-group), and intragroup (one-to-several) levels.

The book will be especially useful for business studies students, junior managers, and people studying communication. Through the use of practical exercises and group discussions, the reader can develop practical skills for use at work.

Lita de Alberdi

1. *perception*

The study of perception in psychology includes seeing, touching, hearing, tasting and smelling. However, for our purposes we shall be concentrating on *person perception*; how we see others and how they see us.

If we are to get on with other people we need to know what they are likely to do, so that we can coordinate our own behaviour with theirs; that is, so that we can behave appropriately in the situation. In any social setting – a discussion with the boss, meeting a person for the first time, a meeting – it is essential to behave in the most appropriate way if we are to succeed and to get the most out of the interaction.

The first thing to bear in mind is that perception is an *active*, *dynamic* process. How we see events varies according to who is looking, and what they expect to see. This depends on things like past experience and how the event is presented. In other words, people vary a great deal.

When we see something happen it can be only too easy to draw the wrong conclusion about what we think is happening because of some *perceptual biases* to which we are prone. If we know about these biases, then we can watch out for them in everyday life and even use them to our advantage in business situations.

general principles

Before we look at specific topics, it is important to be aware of some general principles involved in perception.

1

perception is selective

What we do in any given situation will depend upon what we think is going on. Clearly, we cannot pay attention to everything that we see, hear, smell, etc. Instead we select what we want to concentrate on and screen out those things that we consider to be irrelevant.

Next time you are in a crowded room, such as the canteen, try listening to the conversation of a group near you. You will find that you can hear what they are saying, and that your mind will tend to filter out all the rest of the hubbub going on. If you then concentrate on the general noise, you will not be able to hear the individual conversations around you.

So the first thing we know about perception is that it is *selective* – we choose what we wish to pay attention to. However, this choice is not always under our voluntary control. (See 'Stereotyping', on page 10.)

perception is organised

In many situations we only have incomplete information. From this information we can 'fill in the gaps' to form a complete picture. This general principle is relevant to everything we perceive. For instance, if you show a friend an incomplete picture, for example of a circle that is not joined up, and ask the friend to draw it, he or she will probably draw a complete circle. Psychologists call this the *principle of closure*.

We are always trying to organise what we perceive into wholes. This principle carries over into our thinking about the world as well. When a piece of information is missing, we tend to 'fill in' the gaps, or go beyond the information given.

A second way in which we organise our perception is by *grouping* or *classifying*. Again, this is a result of our being constantly exposed to too much information. To reduce it down to a manageable level, we tend to put things into categories. We see the things in the categories as being roughly the same and do not pay too much attention to detail.

There are two important principles in the classification of things. The first is called the *principle of similarity*; that is, if things look the same we tend to group them together. Look at this line:

ooooooooocccccxxxxxxxxxoooooooooooooooocccccccc

Here we see a group of o's followed by a group of c's followed by a group of x's, and so on.

Now consider the line below:

oooocccc   cccxxxxxxxxxooooo   ooooooooocccc

Here we see three groups; instead of grouping the similar figures together, we group them on the basis of how physically close together they are. This second principle of classification is known as the *principle of proximity*. We do this with people too, as we shall see later in the chapter.

figure and ground

The last principle of perception concerns figure and ground. Whatever we look at we tend to organise into a *figure* – that is, something which stands out – and *ground* – the background against which we see the figure. Looking at Fig. 1, we can reverse the black-and-white figures: we either see two people face to face, or we see a vase.

Fig. 1

This carries over into person perception. We see the person we are considering as the figure and the situation he or she is in as the ground. Because of this tendency we are biased towards attributing that person's behaviour to some aspect of character and not to the situation. Thus the most distinctive feature (the figure) is the focus of our attention. Attribution theory has explored in more detail how it is that we sometimes attribute the cause of someone's behaviour to the person (*dispositional attribution*) and sometimes attribute it to the situation that the person is in (*situational attribution*).

3

attribution theory

In attribution theory, one important source of bias has been identified and is referred to as the *fundamental attribution error*. This refers to the tendency to blame the person for his or her behaviour in a situation, rather than considering whether there was something about the situation that caused the person to behave in that way. However, if we are the actor in the situation, we tend to attribute the cause of our own behaviour to the situation and not to ourselves.

summary

The main principles involved in perception are

- ► SELECTIVITY
- ► ORGANISATION
- ► GROUPING
- ► FIGURE AND GROUND

These principles underlie the topics discussed in this chapter.

person perception

This section is all about how it is that we come to like one person and to dislike another. In the world of work it is not essential that the boss should like you, but it helps! If people like you they are more likely to pay attention to what you say and they are more likely to allocate the resources you need. They are also likely to be more open to being influenced by you since they presumably value your friendship and will not want to lose it.

Bear in mind that at work it can be hard to tell if someone does really like you. For example, subordinates tend to agree with the boss and to be pleasant to him or her.

How do we go about getting people to like us? And how is it that we like some people and not others? How can we avoid making mistakes in our judgement of others?

Argyle (1988) lists seven sources of error in person perception:

1 *Assuming that a person will behave in the same way in any situation* Too much emphasis is laid on the characteristics of the

person, and too little on the influence of the situation in determining that person's behaviour.

2 *Trying too hard to build up a consistent picture of the other person* An assumption is made that if someone has one good/ bad characteristic then he or she will have others; for example, we tend to assume that if someone is generous, he or she is also unselfish, but this is not necessarily true (see Stereotyping on pages 10–12).

3 *Being over-influenced by first impressions – especially physical appearance and accent* (see pages 6 and 11).

4 *Tending to be too positive towards people who are similar to ourselves* For example, people who are from a similar background, school, social class, ethnic grouping (see page 9).

5 *Taking too much notice of the negative side of other people and not looking for their positive features.*

6 *Making constant errors whereby everyone is seen as aggressive, second-rate, etc.*

7 *Not being sufficiently interested in others* (see below).

rewards

If you want the other person to go away with a positive attitude towards you, the first thing to bear in mind is that they need to find that interacting with you is a rewarding and positive experience.

Dale Carnegie wrote a best-seller in the early 1950s called *How to Win Friends and Influence People*, in which he gives six basic rules for how to get people to like you:

1 Become genuinely interested in other people (see (7) in the list above). In other words, stop just thinking about yourself and what you want, and consider what the other person needs too.

2 Smile.

3 Remember that a person's name is to that person the sweetest and most important sound in the English language.

4 Be a good listener. Encourage others to talk about themselves.

5 Talk in terms of the other person's interest.

6 Make the other person feel important – and do it sincerely.

If we think about what Carnegie is saying, each of his rules leads to a form of reward for the other person. By being interested, smiling, remembering a person's name, listening, showing interest and making the other person feel important, we please him or her. Of course, this all has to be genuine.

Studies have shown (e.g. Jones, Hobbs and Hochenburg, 1982) that lonely people are less attentive to their conversational partners. By giving rewards or reinforcement in conversation we are more likely to be seen as being interested in those we are talking to, as well as being warm, friendly and understanding (Hargie, Saunders and Dickson, 1987).

physical appearance

ATTRACTIVENESS

When people are asked if physical attractiveness influences whether or not they like other people, they generally say it does not. However, many studies in psychology have shown that this is not the case. We all like to think that we are rational and reasonable and consider that we should *not* be influenced by factors such as physical attractiveness, but research shows that attractiveness is a very important factor, especially when we first meet people.

Dion, Berscheid and Walster (1972) asked some college students to look at photographs of men and women and to guess their personal characteristics. The more attractive individuals were seen as being more sensitive, kind, strong, interesting, modest and sociable than those who were less attractive.

In another study, students were specially trained to persuade other students to sign a petition in favour of vegetarian meals in the canteen. Those persuaders who were more attractive were able to get more support for their petition than those who were less attractive.

Clearly then, attractiveness is an important source of bias in the perception of others. We tend to think more favourably about attractive people and to attribute favourable characteristics to them. This type of thinking is called the *halo effect*; that is, owing to our tendency to look for wholeness and to organise our perceptions, we think that 'good' characteristics go together. So if an attractive person creates a favourable first impression, we tend then to look out for 'good' characteristics and to ignore 'bad' characteristics, and vice versa (principle of closure).

This can be important in business: interviewing candidates for a job could be biased by the effects of attractiveness, and the recipient of a salesman's attentions could similarly be influenced by his appearance. It could be profitable to employ attractive personnel in the 'front line' of a business; it is not unusual for businesses to have attractive people on reception, where clients first form an impression of the business.

Although you may not see yourself as being physically attractive, one study (Wilson and Nias, 1976) found that attractiveness for females included several elements which are under voluntary control. For example, attractive women in our society should have 'vital statistics' 36-24-35, have regular features, a clear skin and a ready smile, be clean and well groomed, wear fashionable clothes, be healthy and vivacious. In men, attractiveness is not as important, but being tall can be advantageous (see chapter 4), and a man should be clean and well groomed.

GROUP DISCUSSION

Think of as many situations as you can where customers / clients meet someone from a company for the first time. Discuss whether it would be profitable to employ attractive personnel for these positions, and whether it is ethical to employ people on this basis.

DRESS

Although we are not all blessed with a 'pretty face', we can all ensure that we are dressed attractively and appropriately. Will doing so make any difference to our chances in the world? The simple answer is 'Yes'.

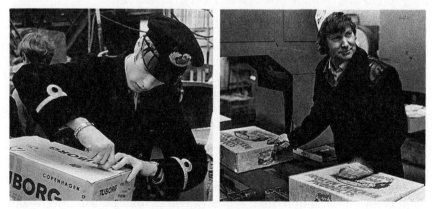

Items of dress suitable for particular jobs

The key thing is to dress *appropriately* for the job in hand. In January 1988 the *Sunday Times* carried an article showing the different types of clothing considered appropriate for different jobs. For example, an insurance salesman commented,

'A suit at all times is what's expected, since we are often dealing with large quantities of money from our policyholders and advising them on important financial decisions. It is right that we should look responsible so that people do not feel they are handing their money over to incompetent cowboys.'

This salesman recognises the importance of inspiring confidence in his clients by dressing for the part. If he were to turn up in jeans and a T-shirt, it is unlikely that he could inspire confidence in his abilities as a financial adviser.

Essentially, dressing for the part is the critical thing here. If you are going for an interview as an accountant and you turn up in ragged jeans and a dirty sweater, it is unlikely that you will be successful! Study what successful people in the sort of job you want are wearing, and develop your own style based on them. By doing this you make yourself credible and get off to a good start. What you wear will not by itself make all the difference but it will create the right atmosphere for success.

GROUP DISCUSSION

Split into small groups of three or four people. Spend ten minutes listing occupations and putting each occupation into one of two categories: those in which appearance is very important, and those in which appearance is not important. Come together as a large group and compare lists. Discuss what is appropriate dress for interviews for two jobs from each list.

competence

We cannot all be beautiful people, but we can strive to be good at our job. We all profess to admire highly competent people, but the evidence from psychological studies is mixed. For example, in problem-solving groups the people with the best ideas are not always the best liked.

One study (Aronson Willerman and Floyd, 1966) investigated competence and found that a highly competent person was liked more than an incompetent one. But interestingly they also found that a highly competent person who made a blunder was liked more than one who did not make a blunder. Perhaps that blunder made the highly competent person more 'human', and therefore more likeable. However, the incompetent person who also made a blunder was liked least of all. Perhaps it was the last straw – not only was this person incompetent, he (or she) had to go and prove it too!

So it definitely pays to be good at your job – but remember to be human too.

first impressions count

The old saying that 'first impressions count' is definitely borne out by research. In psychology this effect is called *primacy*; that is, early-presented information has an undue influence on judgement.

In 1946, Asch carried out an experiment in which he asked people to evaluate someone on the basis of a list of adjectives describing that person's character. To one group he described the person to be evaluated as intelligent, industrious, impulsive, critical, stubborn, envious. To the other group he described the person to be evaluated as envious, stubborn, critical, impulsive, industrious, intelligent. Although the adjectives in both lists are identical, the first group formed a far more favourable impression of the person described than the second group did. The first few adjectives set the tone.

It seems that once people have formed a judgement about another person, they pay little attention to later information received. This is why it is often said that the first five minutes of an interview are critical.

Primacy effects can be counteracted if people are made aware of them and instructed not to make snap judgements and to take all information into account before making a judgement.

similarity

Does like attract like, or do opposites attract? Overall the research supports the popular concept that 'birds of a feather flock together'.

But beware! Although people tend to like those who are similar to them, it seems that this similarity acts as a kind of filter – if someone is similar then we will make the effort to get to know them, but similarity alone does not guarantee that the relationship will continue to prosper. Also, the research seems to show that a certain type of similarity is important – that is, a psychological similarity: people like those who see the world and classify it in similar ways to themselves.

reciprocal liking

We tend to like people who seem to like us. Look back to Carnegie's six rules for getting people to like you (page 5). By acting in the way he recommends, we are acting as if we like the other person. When we like someone we tend to smile when we see them, pay attention to what they are saying, and are interested in them as people.

Studies have shown (e.g. Walster, 1965) that when we are feeling bad about ourselves we tend to like those who like us even more. It is reassuring when one's ego has taken a dent to find that people do still like you – it boosts your confidence.

stereotyping

Forming accurate perceptions of others is important in all social situations because we need to know how to handle them, to be able to predict how they might react.

Impressions of others are often based on *stereotypes*. Stereotypes represent a group of beliefs about a particular type of person. They very often have no basis in fact. Not all stereotypes are negative – there are stereotypes for almost every category of people, for example librarians, engineers, professors, old people, people who drive Porsches, people who jog, and so on.

People who stereotype others are unable to see the individual differences and variability amongst members of a group. This can be a big disadvantage in any situation where accurate assessment of others is required, e.g. as a manager, as a personnel officer, as a nurse, and so on.

Stereotypes are the result of a constant perceptual process described earlier in the chapter – that of *grouping*. People tend to group facts or information into a pattern. This tendency is so strong that people will look for and find patterns where they do not exist; they 'fill in the gaps'. A second process is relevant here too – we tend to force incoming information to fit into preconceived beliefs, beliefs we already hold, and this makes us prey to distortion of the incoming information. We may filter the information we receive and only allow in the facts that fit with our own theories about the world – so we only pay attention to information that confirms an existing belief, and ignore conflicting information.

A stereotype is a type of *schema*. Berkowitz (1986) defined a schema as '. . . a cognitive structure consisting of the perceiver's knowledge and beliefs pertaining to some domain of content'. *Cognitive* means that we are talking about something in the mind, so he means a mental structure which contains an individual's beliefs and knowledge about a particular topic.

Cohen (1981) carried out an experiment to investigate how stereotypes can affect memory for facts about other people. Participants in the experiment were told that they were going to watch a videotape of either a librarian or a waitress. The video was specially designed so that the woman they saw (who was eating and talking with her husband) possessed characteristics that were known to go with the stereotypes of one or other of these occupations. There were nine of each: for example, she wore glasses, played the piano, had been to Europe – all stereotypical characteristics of a librarian; she liked pop music and went bowling – which were seen as stereotypical characteristics of a waitress. Cohen found that when he tested the participants' memory of the woman's characteristics, if they had been told she was a librarian they tended to remember more stereotypical librarian characteristics, and if they had been told that she was a waitress they remembered more stereotypical waitress characteristics, although all the participants had seen the same videotape. So participants remembered information that was consistent with the stereotype they had in mind, and ignored information that was irrelevant.

Stereotypes do not have to be a 'bad thing', because they are useful as a way of summarising groups. They therefore do have their uses, but the point is not to let yourself be carried away by stereotypes, and to pay attention to *all* the information you receive about another person.

Stereotypes can be based on occupation, race, sex, social class or even accent, and can be a dangerous source of bias in person perception.

GROUP DISCUSSION

Consider the following types of people:

football supporters	journalists
rat catchers	secretaries
grave diggers	lecturers
Irishmen	students at Eton
psychologists	feminists

Independently, list two characteristics of each type of person. Put the lists together as a group – do you notice any similarities? Notice if you tend to stereotype any particular type of person more than another. Why?

summary

- ▸ We tend to be biased in our perception of other people.
- ▸ People like to get something out of interacting with us, so we should remember to reward them.
- ▸ Attractive people are seen more positively than unattractive people.
- ▸ Physical appearance is important (dress carefully).
- ▸ We should strive to be good at a job (but remember to be human).
- ▸ First impressions carry a lot of weight.
- ▸ We like those who seem to like us (so beware of flatterers)!
- ▸ Stereotyping is a dangerous source of bias in person perception.

PRACTICAL EXERCISE – *Getting to know you*

What you will need

▶ *Three willing helpers (choose people who are* not *doing the same course)*
▶ *A quiet room where you can talk undisturbed for 20–30 minutes*
▶ *A pen for each of the other three participants*
▶ *A watch or clock*
▶ *Three copies of the rating scales shown below (fill in the blank spaces with your own name)**

**Pages 13 and 14 may be photocopied free of charge for use within the institution that purchases this publication. Photocopies remain the copyright of Cambridge University Press, and may not be used or distributed in any way outside the purchasing institution.*

Rating scales

To be completed at the end of the exercise

Please give .... a score out of 10 for each of the following qualities. 10 means that .... scores highly on the quality and 0 would mean that .... does not have this quality at all. Please try to complete each score as honestly as possible.

Quality	Score out of 10
Fun to be with	....
Interested in others	....
Kind	....
Intelligent	....
Easy to get on with	....
Likeable	....

'I have asked you to come along today to help me with a project on how people get to know each other, which is part of my business studies course. For the next ten minutes I would like you to imagine that we are strangers who have just met. The idea is to exchange information about ourselves. Are you ready to begin? I will tell you when the ten minutes is up.'

What to do

● *When you have chosen three willing helpers, ask the first one to come to the room with you and read out these instructions:*
● *During the ten minutes, try to put into practice the six rules for getting people to like you. That is, respond to what the other person says, show interest, listen carefully, smile at appropriate places, ask questions about his or her interests and listen to the answers, use the person's first name. Focus on the other person.*

- *When the ten minutes are up, ask your helper to fill in the Rating Scales questionnaire.*
- *Explain to your helper what you were really doing and ask him or her not to tell the other two helpers until you have had a session with each of them.*
- *Repeat the process with your second helper, but this time do not put into practice the rules for getting people to like you. Do not show interest in what is said, do not smile. Spend some time talking about yourself.*
- *Repeat the process with your third helper, but this time just be yourself. Try to forget everything you know about getting people to like you and just act naturally for the ten minutes.*

Now total your score for each questionnaire. Compare the marks your helpers gave you.
- *What differences do you notice?*
- *Did your helper like you more when you tried to put the rules into practice? If not, ask your helper about it.*
- *How did you do when you were just being yourself? If you did as well as when you were trying to put the rules into practice, or better, you have nothing to worry about. If you did worse than when you were using the rules, what can you learn from this?*
- *How could you improve your own techniques?*

---

from *People, Psychology and Business* © Cambridge University Press 1990

suggestions for further reading

Argyle, M. (1988) *The Psychology of Interpersonal Behaviour*, Penguin Books, Harmondsworth. A fairly technical book, but a good read if you find you want to know more about this particular area of psychology.

Carnegie, D. (1971) *How to Win Friends and Influence People*, Chaucer Press, Bungay, Suffolk. An interesting read in a chatty style.

Hayes, N. and **Orrell, S.** (1987) *Psychology: An Introduction*, Longman, London. A textbook for GCSE psychology students covering all the basic aspects of psychology.

2. *non-verbal communication*

'We speak with our vocal organs, but we converse with our whole body.' (Abercrombie, 1968)

Non-verbal communication (NVC) refers to all means of communicating with others that do not involve the written or spoken word; that is, the language of actions, e.g. facial expressions, gestures, bodily positions and movements of the body. Non-verbal communication also includes paralinguistic communication; that is, tone of voice, pauses in speech, length of speaking, rhythm of speech, and so on.

Much of our communication occurs at an unconscious level. We make inferences about the other person's attitude or emotional state even though they do not explicitly tell us about either. We are unaware much of the time that we are sending messages to others, just as we are unaware that we are receiving them. Clearly then some understanding of how we communicate through these subtle means will provide a way of avoiding misunderstandings in interpersonal communication, because we will be able to avoid sending 'wrong' messages. We will also gain some insight into what others may be thinking.

In business the importance of non-verbal communication is acknowledged by many companies who train their salesmen, personnel officers and managers in the effective use of non-verbal behaviour. This chapter describes some of the better researched and understood non-verbal behaviours so that you too can use them to advantage.

general principles

actions speak louder than words

It has been estimated (Birdwhistell, 1970) that in a typical two-person interaction the verbal or spoken communication between them conveys about one-third of the meaning of the situation, whilst the non-verbal communication conveys about two-thirds of the meaning. The old song 'It's not what you do but the way that you do it' carries a great deal of basic truth.

the role of non-verbal communication (NVC)

1 NVC can replace speech in certain situations. For example, deaf-and-dumb people communicate via sign language; divers and race-course touts use gestures to communicate.

2 NVC complements speech. The non-verbal component often tells us more about the emotional state of the person. For example, we smile broadly when pleased, or gasp when surprised, or raise our eyebrows to show amazement or to show interest.

3 NVC can help clarify speech. For example, when describing shapes we often describe a shape in the air to clarify the verbal description we are giving.

4 By stressing certain words, or pausing, we can use NVC to lay emphasis on certain words or phrases. This is rather like using capital letters or italics in written communication.

5 Non-verbal signals serve to regulate conversation. Duncan and Fiske (1977) discuss several cues which allow people to identify when it is their turn to speak, for example when the speaker finishes a clause with a rise or fall in voice pitch, or a drop in the volume of the voice.

6 Non-verbal behaviour can provide feedback to people in a conversation. For example, we might notice that a particular line of questioning is causing an employee to act uncomfortably; we can use this information to either drop the subject or pursue it if we feel this is important, depending on the situation.

7 NVC can structure the nature of the relationship between people. For example, Hargie, Saunders and Dickson (1987:12) give the following example:

'If a person wants to influence another by being dominant over him he can manipulate his nonverbal behaviour in order to bring this about. Consider the following behaviours as aspects of dominant nonverbal cues: a louder voice, greater amount of talk, choosing a focal position in a room, standing on a raised dais, sitting behind a desk, sitting at the head of the table, occupying a more impressive chair, interrupting successfully when another person talks, and using long glances to establish a dominant relationship.'

It is thus partially through non-verbal communication that our role in a relationship is established and maintained.

Hence, rather than actually stating that you do not like someone or that you wish to take control of the interaction, these can be achieved by the manipulation of non-verbal signals. Successful leaders use these techniques all the time.

Finally, it is important to bear in mind that non-verbal behaviours vary across different cultures and societies. The content of this chapter is directed at residents of the UK and USA in particular. Some behaviours, although they look similar, in fact mean something quite different in different cultures – so beware. For example, the Japanese are taught from an early age that it is shameful to express negative emotions in public, so even in distressing situations the Japanese keep on smiling or at least do not show that they are upset; hence their reputation for being inscrutable – they are!

non-verbal behaviours

touching

The amount and type of touching which is acceptable varies according to sex and society. Although touching in Western society is restricted, people who do touch others are often very popular, which suggests that a certain amount of touching can be useful.

For example, one study (Fisher, Rytting and Hesling, 1975) showed that if librarians touched the hand of readers returning cards, the female readers who were touched liked both the librarians and the library better than those who were not touched. The contact only lasted for about half a second, but this was enough. So touching signals friendliness and warmth. This is very simple to put into practice – when handing things to other people, just ensure that you brush their hand as you do so. This can be especially useful when you are interviewing or are being interviewed, in order to establish rapport with the other person.

Another study (Henley, 1977) investigated touch between high- and low-status individuals. They found that high-status people tend to touch low-status people, for example by putting an arm across their shoulder, but that low-status people do not initiate touching; instead they allow the higher-status person to touch them. Touch, then, can signal status in an interaction. By touching the other person you can signal that you do not consider yourself to be of a lower status and that you are a warm and friendly person.

personal space

Linked to touch is the space that surrounds our bodies – our personal space or personal zone. One reason that we do not touch continuously is that we surround ourselves with invisible barriers which others cross at their peril.

Personal space varies according to the culture we live in. Arabs and Latin Americans stand very close, whilst Swedes and Scots are the most distant.

The more intimate our relationship with another person, the closer we will allow him or her to come. However, how close people can approach to us also varies according to the situation we are in.

Hall (1966) distinguished four main zones according to the nature of the interaction taking place (Fig. 2):

Fig.2   Zones of interaction

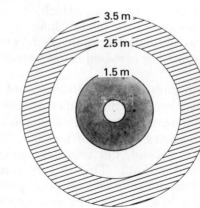

Public zone

Social zone

Personal zone

Intimate zone

3.5 m
2.5 m
1.5 m

1 *Intimate zone*   This is about 18 inches (45 cm) – people with an intimate relationship will stand at about this distance when talking.

2 *Personal zone*   This is from about 18 inches (45 cm) from each other to 4 feet (1.5 m) and is the distance we put between ourselves and friends.

3 *Social zone*   This is about 9 to 12 feet (2.5 to 3.5 m) and is the comfortable distance for conducting business with others.

4 *Public zone*   Public speakers and lecturers usually put at least 12 feet (3.5 m) between themselves and their audience.

At work, it is usually appropriate to keep about 9 feet (2.5 m) between yourself and a client. Getting too close will signal hostility and dominance. Think of the boss who walks into your office and leans over your desk – this invasion helps to confirm the boss's right to invade your space. On the other hand, when you enter the boss's office, do you find that you hover by the door? This is because it is difficult to enter another's personal space if you think that he or she is the dominant person. If you move too close you will make the other person feel uncomfortable, even threatened. He or she will express this by moving away, or if this is not possible, signal non-verbally by turning away or looking away, and so on.

People who stand too far away, on the other hand, are seen as standoffish, aloof and cold. It is important to maintain the right distance between you and those whom you meet if you want to have a comfortable and productive interaction with them, and this is particularly important in work settings.

PRACTICAL EXERCISE

Investigating personal space

The object of this exercise is to examine personal space in different situations. You will need paper and a pen, and a keen eye. You may also need a certain amount of tact.

For the less assertive: *Visit three locations in which people gather for different purposes, for example a pub, the canteen, the library, a public meeting. Observe those around you as they talk and interact. You should be able to observe two interesting things:*
1 the amount of space (if any!) between two people, and
2 how much their gestures are similar to each other.
(See 'Gestures', page 21.)

Having made your observations, you will find that people in intimate situations sit closer together than those having a discussion about work, and also that they tend to mirror each other's gestures.

Come together as a group and discuss your findings. What other non-verbal cues were useful as indicators of the type of relationship that your 'victims' were involved in?

For the brave: *Proceed as above. Work with another person, find some suitable locations, and find a good vantage point. Now, the braver person should start moving in on the people who are being observed. How do they react? You should find invisible barriers which, when crossed, will cause your 'victim' or 'victims' to become uncomfortable. Where are these barriers? Do they differ between men and women?*

Come together as a group and discuss your findings.

orientation

Orientation means the *angle* at which we interact with others. We tell others something of what we expect when we position ourselves in a room.

Imagine that A in Fig. 3 is sitting at a table. B has several choices of position in which to seat himself.

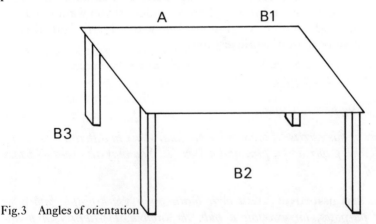

Fig.3   Angles of orientation

If B chooses position B1, then he sees the situation as being one of cooperation; B2 means that he thinks that the situation is one of competing, negotiating or selling to A. He may also choose this position in which to interview A. B3 signals that B sees the situation as a discussion or conversation.

It is, then, significant where we sit. Even before we speak we can tell others a great deal about our intentions in a situation. What position should we choose for which situation?

B1 would be appropriate if you are working with a colleague on a project; B2 is for formal job interviews or situations where you want to keep the other person on their toes; B3 is good for counselling interviews, less formal job interviews and boss/employee discussions.

GROUP DISCUSSION

Form into groups of three or four people and consider the topic of orientation. What does the group feel would be the optimum / best orientation for:
- *a boss who wants to discipline a problem employee?*
- *a boss who is trying to help an employee with personal problems?*
- *someone wanting to discuss arrangements for the visit of an important client with a colleague who is well-known for being obstructive and difficult to deal with?*

Come together as a group after 10 minutes. Does the group agree? How do the three situations differ? Is orientation equally important in all three situations?

---

gestures

Each culture has a range of gestures which are understood by everyone within that culture. Consider the following from Western culture: clenched fist, beckoning finger, waving hand, pointing finger, clapping hands. The meaning of each is clear to us.

When a person speaks, he or she uses gestures to illustrate what is being said, rather like a running non-verbal commentary. Such gestures are called *illustrators*. These are important because they serve to increase the clarity and comprehension of spoken communication. Also, it has been found that when interviewers, public speakers and salesmen use illustrators they can get and keep the attention of their audience by showing their enthusiasm and making the interaction more interesting and enjoyable for participants. So do not be afraid to use your body to add to what you are saying.

Gestures also tell us a great deal about the emotional state of the other person. For example, a nervous interviewee may wring the hands, fidget the fingers by fiddling with objects or hair, wriggle or curl the toes – such involuntary gestures of the extremities (hands and feet) are known as *leakage* because the true feelings 'leak out' at the edges. Embarrassment is shown by a hand over the mouth, anger by clenched hands, and shame by covering the eyes.

When we like someone we tend to use more *open* gestures than when we do not. Open gestures are those which do not create barriers between ourselves and others. Thus crossed arms and crossed legs both signal that we are unsure / uneasy / defensive / do not like the other person, and are called *closed* gestures.

Significant gestures

posture

The way in which we sit or stand is a good indicator of the way we *feel*. Whilst facial expression can signal *which* emotion is being felt, posture can indicate the *degree* to which the emotion is felt (Ekman and Friesen, 1967). So, for example, a drooping body posture can show that a person is very depressed, while a taut, upright position might show extreme anxiety.

Posture is also closely linked with perceptions of *status*. When sitting, the higher-status person tends to adopt a more casual posture than the low-status person. When standing, the high-status individual tends to be more relaxed, perhaps with hands in the pockets, whilst the lower-status person is stiffer and straighter.

Posture also conveys a positive or negative attitude to the other person. Siegal (1980) found that if a seated person leans towards another person, he or she is seen as having a more positive attitude towards both the other person and the subject under discussion. If the two people are standing, then to show a positive attitude one person must face directly towards the other.

When people have a conversation, the listener often unconsciously copies the movements of the speaker, as well as the posture. This seems to be a signal of empathy and interest. You can observe this quite easily. Try going to the pub and watching people in conversation; you will soon observe this postural echoing. Try doing it yourself – surprisingly people don't notice that you are doing it, but you should find that it puts them at ease, although they won't know why.

It is as well to know these signs, especially if you are involved in selling, or in any area of business like interviewing, or even just working with others in a team. These gestures give useful clues to how you are being evaluated by the other person, how he or she is receiving what you are saying, and how the other person is feeling.

facial expression

One of the main ways of showing emotion is through facial expression. There are seven main expressions: happiness, surprise, fear, sadness, anger, disgust or contempt, and interest. The mouth and the eyebrows are particularly important in communicating emotions. For example, Argyle (1988) discusses the different meanings of various positions of the eyebrows:

fully raised – disbelief   half lowered – puzzled
half raised – surprise   fully lowered – angry
normal – no comment

Of course, many people are skilled at controlling their facial expressions, and thus it is not always such a good indicator as other non-verbal behaviours.

Examples of facial expressions

Facial expression is a valuable source of feedback to a speaker and can indicate that others are listening and interested. Certainly those who do not change their facial expression are seen as odd or not 'normal'.

One study found that we are far more expressive on the left side of our face than on the right. By cutting photographs in two and creating mirror images to form a face made of either two left sides or two right sides, it was found that the left-side photos were more expressive than the right-side photos. This is probably because the right side of the brain – which controls the left side of the face – is primarily concerned with emotional and intuitive tasks.

eye gaze and eye contact

The importance of eyes in dealing with others is demonstrated by the large number of common remarks about them. For example, 'He's got shifty eyes' (I don't trust him); 'She's making eyes at me' (She fancies me); 'I felt that he was looking right through me' (He wasn't interested in what I was saying).

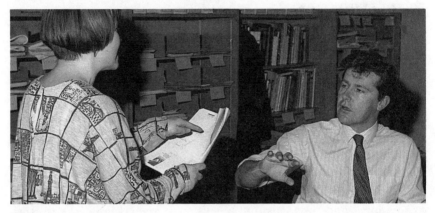

Two people in conversation

When we are in conversation with another person, eye gaze and eye contact have a very important role. Argyle (1978), summarising research in this area, asserts that 'When two people are talking, they look at each other between 25% and 75% of the time . . . They look nearly twice as much while listening as while talking.' Argyle and Ingham (1972) found that listeners looked at the speaker 75% of the time and the speaker looked at the listener 41% of the time. Kendon (1967) also found that people looked for a longer period when they were listening than when they were talking. Beattie (1981) argues that this is because the speaker needs to shut out any distractions while he is thinking about what he is saying. Also, the speaker needs to get feedback on how his message is being received and therefore needs to look at the listener for non-verbal signals.

Studies have shown that the weaker of two people in conversation looks more at the dominant person. It is thought that this signals that the weaker person accepts his or her position and that the weaker looks more to gain feedback, which is more important for him or her than for the dominant person. We also know that we tend to look less at people whom we dislike than at people we like.

In groups, the dominant person usually seats him- or herself in such a way as to be able to see all the other group members. Also, if a new group is seated in a room, the person who happens to be in such a position often becomes the leader.

The topic of conversation is also important. If the content is personal, as in a personal evaluation, we prefer the speaker to look away more when the evaluation is good, but if the evaluation is bad we prefer the speaker to look more at us. When the evaluation is not personal but is bad, we prefer the speaker to look away. If the topic under discussion is difficult then people look less, as they do when the topic is intimate.

Eyes also serve as regulators for speech. When the speaker holds the floor for a long time, he will glance at the other person to check that it is all right to continue; the listener signals by a nod or a grunt that she is happy for the speaker to continue. When the speaker is ready to stop speaking he looks at the listener as if to say, 'Over to you . . .'

Eye gaze is also used to begin a conversation – we 'catch the eye' of the other person who signals readiness (or otherwise) to converse with us.

Overall, then, eye gaze allows people to check others for their reaction. It helps to keep conversation going, it provides signals about when it is your turn to speak, and it signals something about the way the content of the conversation is viewed by the participants.

Argyle (1988) summarises what it may mean if A looks at B a great deal:

1 They are placed a long way apart. If we are quite a way from the other person, we look more at them.

2 They are discussing impersonal or easy topics.

3 There is nothing else to look at. People look at each other less if they are discussing something concrete, like a document or a map, for example.

4 A is interested in B and in B's reactions.

5 A likes or loves B.

6 A is of a lower status than B.

7 A is trying to dominate or influence B. Before dominance is established in a relationship, the person who is trying to achieve dominance will look more until his or her higher status is established, then will look less.

8 A is an extrovert. Extroverts – that is, sociable, happy-go-lucky, gregarious people – do tend to look more at others, presumably to confirm that they are liked, since this is very important to extroverts, who value relationships.

paralinguistics

Paralinguistics refers to the study of the non-verbal aspects of speech such as tone of voice, pauses, rhythm of speech and pitch of voice.

Giles and Powesland (1975) showed that different accents have different levels of prestige attached to them. For example, in the UK the standard 'received pronunciation' is the most prestigious, and the Birmingham and Cockney accents are the least prestigious.

The paralinguistic aspects of speech help us to detect emotion. For example, Scherer (1979) argues that when people are angry they speak more quickly. When people are anxious or apprehensive they tend to make more errors in their speech.

Pauses occur frequently during conversations, and research has shown that people vary in their reactions to pauses; some cannot tolerate them and talk to fill in the gaps, while others can tolerate quite long pauses. Newman (1982) suggests that if strangers or acquaintances have long pauses in their conversations they become uncomfortable. Probably the better we know someone, the more likely we are to tolerate pauses without feeling worried by them.

Varying the tone and pace of your speech can help to make it more interesting to other people. If you drone away you will soon notice that others have trouble maintaining interest in what you are talking about. So it is a good idea to vary pace, tone and pitch to keep others listening to you.

GROUP DISCUSSION

Form into groups of three or four people. Each group should choose three work situations, for example:
- *disciplinary interview*
- *giving a presentation to the Board*
- *keeping control of a group of lively and difficult colleagues.*

Consider how non-verbal behaviour can help to achieve goals in each situation.

---

some conclusions

If you want to show another person that you are friendly, try using some or all of the following:

touch	frequent looking
nearness	smiling
side-by-side orientation	soft, warm tone of voice
leaning towards the other	open gestures

summary

- Non-verbal communication is an important component of most interactions.
- Non-verbal behaviour is different in different cultures.
- Touching can signal warmth or status.
- Personal space surrounds us all; when invaded we can become uneasy.
- Our orientation to others reveals the type of interaction we expect to follow.
- Gestures can signal how we feel in a situation.
- Posture is also an indicator of mood and attentiveness.
- Facial expression is one of the main ways in which we show emotion.
- Eye gaze and eye contact serve to regulate conversations and can be used to establish dominance.

suggestions for further reading

Bull, P. (1983) *Body Movement and Interpersonal Communication*, John Wiley and Sons Ltd, London. An excellent and comprehensive discussion of all aspects of non-verbal behaviour.

Fast, J. (1971) *Body Language*, Pan, London. A light read – fun sections on the language of love and how to 'fake' body language.

3. *motivation*

When we talk about motivation, we mean the impetus of our behaviour; that is, the energy which directs and propels us into action, and also sustains that action. At work, motivation is the force that keeps us going and drives us on to complete the job at hand.

Motivation presents a problem in the world of work, a problem that is relevant when recruiting staff, managing staff and when being an effective worker in an organisation. When as a manager you take people on you hope that they will be motivated to do the job well. How to find this out is discussed first in this chapter. Secondly, we look at a major problem for managers: that of motivating employees to work consistently and effectively at the tasks they are set to complete. Finally, we look at the problems of how to get yourself going and look at reasons why you might become de-motivated and what you can do about it.

recruitment

We will not look at recruitment *per se*, just at those aspects of it that refer to motivation.

There are various psychometric tests available. These are tests that are used to measure the individual's psychological characteristics such as intelligence, creativity or personality. Many concentrate on the individual's personality. The reason for the popularity of these tests is that they are *objective*; they are supposed to sort out who will fit into an organisation and who will not. Some tests also look at how people interact with others – that is, their social ability – which is especially important in close-knit teams. There are therefore two aspects to testing:

- Will the individual fit into the organisational culture?
- Will the individual fit in with the other people in the organisation?

There are no right or wrong answers to these tests. If you should come across them, *be truthful*, because if you do not fit into the organisation or are not the right type of personality for the team, pretending that you are will be stressful. You are not very likely to be able to keep up the front once you start in the job.

It could be argued that the personality tests will tell you something about an individual's motivation level, but there are problems with these kinds of test. Probably the most serious is that people's responses *vary* – the tests are not reliable over time, and people may say one thing one day and another the next day, depending on their mood, for example. The other problem is the *faking* problem (see above) which is also serious – anyone who takes a psychological test will strive to seem to be hard-working, sensible, etc., particularly if a job hangs on the results. In other words, people try to present themselves in a favourable light at the expense of the truth. So whilst testing is useful and has its place in the recruitment process, we need other ways of assessing applicants' potential to do the job.

So what do we do? The first thing to remember is that people are individuals and have to be approached as such. Recruitment is a very important function in any organisation. Organisations are made up of *people* – they are its single most important resource.

Maslow's needs hierarchy

One theory, put forward by Abraham Maslow (1954), tried to take account of the individuality of people, and concentrated on their *needs*. Maslow argued that people are motivated by their current needs and that these needs are structured hierarchically; that is, we have to satisfy the needs at the bottom of the hierarchy before we can move up to satisfy 'higher needs'.

Maslow grouped needs into five categories. His hierarchy is often drawn as a pyramid with the lowest, most basic needs at the bottom, and the highest, most abstract needs at the top (Fig.4).

Fig.4   Maslow's needs hierarchy

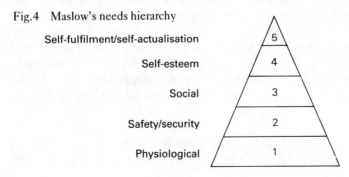

Self-fulfilment/self-actualisation 5

Self-esteem 4

Social 3

Safety/security 2

Physiological 1

1 *Physiological needs*   The needs we have at the most basic level: hunger, thirst, reproduction of the species, and so on. The idea is that if one of these needs is present we will satisfy it before any other of the higher needs. At work, this level would refer to basic working conditions: a decent canteen, toilets, washing facilities.

2 *Safety/security needs*   The need for shelter and security from threat. At work this would mean job security, salary, pensions.

3 *Social needs*   The need to belong to a social group and have friends. At work this would refer to being part of a work group or team, perhaps making friends through the sports and social clubs.

4 *Self-esteem needs*   The need to gain respect from other people and recognition of worth. In a work context this might mean praise from the boss or recognition of a job well done.

5 *Self-fulfilment needs*   The need to fulfil yourself to the best of your potential. Also called self-actualisation needs. At work this would mean needing a stretching and challenging job.

People can 'get stuck' at one of the need levels, perhaps because they have been severely deprived, and may never feel that the need is completely satisfied. Needs will also change over the life cycle. Young people will probably be more concerned with social needs; then when they marry and have a family, security needs will predominate; when the family have grown up then self-esteem and self-actualisation needs may become important.

Finally, needs may vary from culture to culture. For example, in Japan social needs and self-esteem needs are likely to be more important, whereas in the USA self-fulfilment needs are more likely to dominate.

In order to assess what motivates people at work, it is necessary first of all to identify which is the dominant set of needs for each individual, and then to ensure that the job fulfils these needs. The problem here is that it is not clear that by satisfying needs and therefore ensuring job satisfaction we will necessarily ensure a satisfactory level of performance on the job. That is, the link between need satisfaction and job satisfaction has not been definitely established.

The other problem with this approach is that there is insufficient evidence to show that Maslow's five levels of needs analysis is actually correct. For example, it has not been conclusively established that the needs are hierarchically ordered in the way that Maslow conceptualised them.

ERG theory

ERG theory was developed by Alderfer (1972). This theory suggests that there are only three groups of needs which are important: existence (E), relatedness (R), and growth (G). These needs determine people's motivations at work and are also arranged hierarchically, but unlike Maslow's theory, in ERG theory the individual can have more than one set of needs activated at any one time. People can also move up and down the hierarchy.

The three groups of needs are as follows:

1 *Existence needs* These correspond roughly with Maslow's physiological and security needs.

2 *Relatedness needs* These correspond with Maslow's social needs.

3 *Growth needs* These correspond with Maslow's self-esteem and self-fulfilment needs.

needs and recruitment

How are these needs theories useful in recruitment? If we can find out what people's needs are, we are in a better position to see if they are going to enjoy the job in question. So how do we assess a person's needs?

1 *Physiological needs* People with strong physiological needs are likely to apply for jobs in the manual and process sectors. It is difficult to assess them. They may be interested in sports, especially as a spectator. (Haines, 1979)

2 *Safety needs* People with strong safety/security needs fit in best with very structured organisations and strong or authoritarian management styles. They are most common in the 35–55 year-old age group. These people will usually not move jobs often and will be concerned about issues like salary, pensions and job security. They will be attracted to organisations such as banks, insurance companies, building societies, local government or the civil service.

3 *Social needs* People with strong social needs are fairly easy to spot – they spend their spare time in social groups, for example at the pub or in sports and social clubs, and they stress the importance of their friends.

4 *Self-esteem needs* High self-esteem needs are common among middle- and upper-class people who will often seem confident at interviews. They are likely to be attracted by jobs in the professions, academic jobs and as union officials. They may well enjoy the status of such jobs and may use 'I', 'we' and 'me' frequently in conversation.

5 *Self-fulfilment needs* People whose needs are high in this respect often move from jobs once they have mastered them – they seek challenges, and look for high standards in others. They do not make good bosses because they find managing others troublesome. Look for these people in creative positions – artists, writers, film directors – or 'at the top', as sportsmen, consultants, entrepreneurs. An organisation is not likely to need many of these people, but they are very valuable because they are the innovators.

One way to find out how oriented candidates are to achievement is to give them a blank sheet of paper and ask them to write down what they want to achieve in the next five years. Those with a high need for self-fulfilment will have no trouble doing this and may write a great deal; conversely the average manual worker will experience much difficulty with such a task.

Various people have put forward other needs theories, but the three needs which have generated the most attention are the need for *achievement*, the need for *affiliation* and the need for *power*.

1 *The need for achievement* Some people have a high need to achieve, whilst others do not. Those with a high need for achievement will relish a challenge, set themselves high standards, enjoy competition and strive for excellence. These people are the 'self-starters', so often sought in job advertisements. The high achiever usually has a career goal in mind and can be a 'workaholic'.

2 *The need for affiliation* People with a high need for affiliation like other people and enjoy their company; they are friendly and seek out friendships. They are often motivated by the desire for approval from their friends and companions; they are also interested in the thoughts and feelings of others. (See the sections on social needs above.)

3 *The need for power* These are the people who strive to achieve influential positions. They need to attempt to control their environment, both the physical and the social environment. These people usually have strong aspirations for power, status and money.

Matching needs to jobs helps considerably to ensure that employees get what they want out of the job, thus increasing the chances that they will strive to do the job well and will stay in the job.

Other indicators of motivation levels are things like extra-curricular activities at school or college – the organiser of the debating society or the hiking club is likely to be a person who enjoys organising and has plenty of spare energy that can be harnessed at work. Obviously people who look upon their hobbies as being more important than their job are not suitable for management positions, but managers should have plenty of energy and initiative.

Finally, one other indicator of motivation is the person's ability to see things through. Those who have high self-fulfilment needs are easily bored and often do not finish things. If people do stick at things they are likely to continue to do so in the job.

In conclusion, one of the most helpful indicators of motivation is the candidate's enthusiasm for the job. Does he appear to really *want* the job? If so, *why*? Do his or her ideas about what the job entails match the reality? If they don't, this should be explained to the candidate. There is no point in trying to match a square peg to a round hole.

managing

Now the job candidate is the job holder. The manager's job is to motivate subordinates to do the job and continue to do the job to the best of their ability. This section offers some perspectives on how to do this. (See also chapter 4, 'Leadership'.)

reinforcement

This approach is based on the idea of a stimulus and a response. A person responds to a stimulus from the environment. Early theories really only examined *external* stimuli and not internal or self-generated stimuli to behaviour. They were called *behaviourist theories*, and were based on Pavlov's idea of *classical conditioning*.

Pavlov observed that dogs would salivate when they were given food. If he paired the giving of food with the ringing of a bell, eventually, through association, the dogs learned to salivate when they heard the bell, without being fed or offered food. The bell was called the *conditioned stimulus*; the dogs were conditioned to salivate when they heard it. This salivation he called the conditioned response (Fig. 5).

Fig.5

STIMULUS ⟶ leads to ⟶ RESPONSE

Skinner developed a theory called *operant conditioning*, which is another approach to the stimulus response situation. The subject has to operate on the environment to produce the response. In Pavlov's model, the subject (a dog in this case) waited passively for the stimulus and then responded to it. In Skinner's model, the subject has to do something and is then rewarded. The reward can be something pleasant – a positive reinforcer – or it can be the opposite – a punishment which the individual strives to avoid. Negative reinforcement can also be used where the pleasant stimulus is not given, or is taken away if the subject does something which is not wanted.

These ideas of classical and operant conditioning underlie all the theories that emphasise giving people rewards at work. These rewards are often called *incentives* and include things like salary, bonuses, promotions, praise, and so on. The problem with them is that they leave out any characteristics of the person involved, and this is often referred to as the *black box approach* (Fig. 6). The individual is seen as a mysterious black box into which the stimulus disappears, and reappears as the response.

Fig.6

STIMULUS ⟶ BLACK BOX ⟶ RESPONSE

However, leaving the person completely 'undescribed' like this rather oversimplifies things. People are different in all sorts of ways, and contexts and situations also vary. People interpret their environment and the stimuli from it according to the situation in which they find themselves, the norms of the situation, and according to their own attitudes and experience.

If it is used carefully, though, this theoretical perspective can be translated into a work context and can lead to increases in productivity and performance in organisations. It is known as *OB Mod* (*O*rganisational *B*ehaviour *Mod*ification). This approach has been challenged as unethical because it is based on manipulating people, and this criticism should be carefully considered. However, perhaps we should also think about the wider issue of control in organisations. Managers aim to influence those who work for them – is this unethical?

OB Mod has been used quite widely and successfully and involves giving reinforcement when the desired behaviour is evident. Praise and recognition are often used as positive reinforcers, as well as time off and pay. However, results must be viewed with caution, since unsuccessful interventions often pass unreported, and we know that when attention is paid to people they often respond with better productivity just because they enjoy the attention. (This is known as the *Hawthorne effect*.)

Lawler (1977) suggested a number of factors to be considered when designing a reward-based system. First, he said that the rewards used must be *important to the individuals concerned*; secondly, the system must be *flexible* so that the right rewards can be used; thirdly, *enough* of the reward must be used that those on the receiving end stay motivated to strive for it; fourthly, the *connection* between increased performance and the reward must be made clearly enough to ensure that the employees understand that it is there; finally, the *cost* of the rewards must be outweighed by the increased performance of the employees.

If these things are taken into account, such a system may well work. Of course, problems arise when jobs are dependent on each other, as so often happens. In these cases reward systems can be very difficult to design on an individual basis – if they are designed on a group basis there may be many problems in terms of who gets how much, and so on.

To summarise, this approach is based on the idea of rewarding people for their efforts. Studies have shown that it can be effective, but usually it is easier to administer on an individual basis than on a group basis. Remember also that it is more effective to arrange things so that positive reinforcement is used – praise, extra pay or promotion – rather than negative reinforcement or punishment, which research shows is far less effective in changing people's behaviour.

equity theory

Equity theory is quite appealing at commonsense level. It argues that people are motivated by a need to see that they are fairly treated. If they do not feel fairly treated they will be motivated to rectify the situation.

Hence, people will compare how much they put into their job with how much other people put into theirs, and they will want to see that those who are roughly on a par with themselves get the same sorts of reward as they do for the effort expended. Thus in industry, for example, a group of workers from the paint shop may compare themselves with another group of workers, probably but not always from the same company. These sorts of comparison can form the basis of industrial disputes over differentials.

If unfair treatment is found then employees will either reduce their efforts, leave the job, perhaps find others in the organisation to compare themselves with, or pressure their co-workers to work less hard; finally they might distort their own perception and adjust their view by saying to themselves that maybe they just work harder than everyone else.

This is a very brief rundown on equity theory, because basically it is not precise enough to be very useful. It does not say which choice of restoring equity will be chosen in any situation, and it does not seem to take past experience into account at all. However, it reminds us that people think it is important to feel that they are being treated fairly. There are two points to be made here:

1 Managers must try to ensure that everyone is fairly rewarded for their contribution to the organisation.

2 Managers must check that the rewards are *seen* to be fair by all the employees.

Herzberg's motivation–hygiene theory

Herzberg took a very practical approach to motivation. He carried out a study in which he asked people about what made them happy and unhappy at work. He found two groups of factors which were important:

1 *Hygiene/maintenance factors* These were things in the environment which caused dissatisfaction, such as working conditions, salary, job security. Interestingly, these factors can cause a person to feel unhappy, but when the person is unhappy they tend to put this down to the second group of factors.

2 *Motivators* These were things like feelings of achievement, responsibility, or satisfaction at doing the job well.

So it is important that the hygiene factors are satisfactory in order to avoid dissatisfaction. To increase happiness in the job the second group of factors is important. This has led to the idea that job enrichment can give more job satisfaction, responsibility and challenge to the individual. This is not always easy to achieve, especially on the factory floor.

This theory has been criticised for various reasons, one of which is that, like needs theories, it is not clear that happy workers are productive workers; that is, increased job satisfaction may not lead to increased productivity.

What can we get from this approach? First, the basics must be adequately taken care of; people need to work in a decent environment. Secondly, it is important to stress achievement in the job so that people feel they are doing something worthwhile of which they can feel proud.

expectancy theory

This theory was first put forward by Vroom (1964). Later it was developed by Porter and Lawler (1968). It is probably the most popular current theory.

The first type of expectancy is the degree to which people expect that if they put in a certain amount of effort, then they will achieve a certain amount of performance – so a lot of effort means a high level of performance. For example, a student who works hard will expect to perform well in exams. This is put in numerical terms: a value of 1.0 means that you are certain that if you work hard you will perform well, whilst a value of 0.0 means that you think that however hard you work you will not achieve anything. This numerical value expresses the strength of belief about the link between effort put in and performance. A numerical value of 0.0 *should* mean that the student is not motivated to study at all, since he or she does not believe it can help. Thus the higher this effort–performance expectancy value, the more an individual will be motivated to work hard.

The second type of expectancy concerns the relationship between performance and other sorts of outcome, e.g. pay or promotion. Again this is expressed numerically, with 1.0 meaning that you are certain that if you can perform well you will get the desired outcome, and 0.0 meaning that you do not think there is any link at all, so however well you perform you will not get the desired outcome. These outcomes are either *intrinsic* – feeling satisfied, feeling you have met a challenge – or *extrinsic* – pay, promotion, praise. Intrinsic factors come from the person, whilst extrinsic factors come from outside the person. Again, the closer the value is to 1.0, the greater the motivation of the person.

Finally, the outcomes have *valences* associated with them. Valence is the satisfaction or dissatisfaction you expect from the outcomes, and it is this that decides whether you will put in the effort to get the anticipated outcome. So if you were likely to feel dissatisfied with the outcome, you would not be motivated to put the effort in to get it.

Nadler and Lawler (1977) list seven factors which managers should consider as a result of this theory:

1 Work out which outcomes are valued by subordinates.

2 Decide what kind of performance is wanted from subordinates.

3 Make sure that subordinates can attain the desired level of performance.

4 Tie the desired outcomes with the desired performance.

5 Check the situation for any conflicting expectancies.

6 Ensure that the outcomes are seen as sufficient reward.

7 Check that the system is fair.

These recommendations also integrate some factors from reinforcement theories and equity theory. In organisational terms, Nadler and Lawler recommend the following steps:

1 Design pay and reward systems which do reward performance and effort by employees.

2 Design jobs flexibly so that employees' different needs are taken into account and fulfilled.

3 Train managers so that they are able to set clear and achievable goals which are clearly tied in with rewards, thus enabling them to generate a positive motivational level by giving positive reinforcement.

4 Regularly monitor motivational levels throughout the organisation.

5 Make sure that the system is flexible enough to allow employees to choose their own rewards.

investigating attitudes

Managers often say, 'The problem with Z is his attitude.' Sometimes attitude questionnaires can be useful to determine employee morale. Measuring attitudes is a specialised job and is usually carried out by psychologists, since there are several approaches which can be adopted. For example, Bergen (1939) developed a series of statements which can be used to assess the attitudes of employees towards their work organisation (Table 1).

Table 1 *Statements used in Bergen's scale for the measurement of attitudes of employees towards their company*

I am made to feel that I am really a part of this organisation.

I can feel reasonably sure of holding my job as long as I do good work.

I can usually find out how I stand with my boss.

On the whole, the company treats us about as well as we deserve.

I think training in better ways of doing the job should be given to all employees of the company.

I have never understood just what the company personnel policy is.

In my job I don't get any chance to use my experience.

I can never find out how I stand with my boss.

A large number of employees would leave here if they could get as good jobs elsewhere.

I think that the company's policy is to pay employees just as little as it can get away with.

This approach can be especially useful if there seems to be a general problem with morale, and questionnaires can be developed for particular problems.

conclusion

The next chapter, 'Leadership' gives ideas on how to manage others. As a manager, you need to remember that the people who work for you are *people* – treat them like people and not like machines and they will appreciate it. A smile, a friendly word of encouragement, showing interest, and saying 'thank you' go a long way. When things are going well and your people are working hard, say that you are pleased – showing that you appreciate their efforts will make them feel good. Make room in your day for a subordinate with problems; if problems are ignored they get worse and resentments build up.

motivating yourself at work

From the preceding discussion we can see that in order for people to be motivated there are a variety of factors involved. If you wake up 'bright-eyed and bushy-tailed' every morning, leap out of bed and arrive smiling at work looking forward to every minute of it, then don't bother to read on!

If on the other hand you feel that this does not describe you and your attitude to work, we explore here some of the reasons why you may not be performing at your best. First, we have already looked at several theories about motivation, so let's re-examine those in a personal light.

Below is a practical exercise designed to identify personal needs for achievement, affiliation and power. Before you read any further, do the exercise and identify whether you are high or low on these needs.

PRACTICAL EXERCISE – Looking at needs

Read the list of statements below. Using the scale, rate each statement on how important it is to you personally.

5	4	3	2	1
Extremely important	Fairly important	Not very important	Fairly unimportant	Completely unimportant

A *High standards, winning, succeeding, doing well.*
B *Creating, artistic accomplishment, unique achievements.*
C *Having a long-term goal; wanting to do well in a specific career, or being successful in life.*
D *Being on good terms with other people.*
E *Wanting other people to like you.*
F *Seeing other people being happy and being concerned for their well-being.*
G *Being in control of the situation.*
H *Persuading other people.*
I *Being the appointed leader.*

Now add together your scores for statements A, B *and* C. *Next add together your scores for* D, E *and* F. *Finally, total your scores for statements* G, H *and* I. *This gives you three separate totals.*

The score for A + B + C *reflects your need for* **achievement**.
The score for D + E + F *reflects your need for* **affiliation**.
The score for G + H + I *reflects your need for* **power**.
The higher your score for each need, the more important it is to you.

Adapted from Biddle and Evenden, 1980

Now that you have your scores, consider your needs in relation to what you are getting from your job. For example, if you have a high need for power, what steps are you taking to fulfil that need? Or do you have a high need for affiliation? If so, are you in a work environment that brings you into contact with other people?

If you have a mismatch between your needs and what you actually get from your job, then you must act. Talk to your boss – can your job be re-designed to help you fulfil your needs? If not, then you should seriously consider getting another job that can.

If you are not getting what you need from your job, then it is not surprising that you are not motivated to work hard because you cannot see that the outcomes from your effort are worth striving for.

Turning to behaviourist approaches, do you get praise for what you do? Or do you feel undervalued and unappreciated? If so, then again, a word with your boss may not go amiss.

From the expectancy theory viewpoint, it may be that you are not clear on just what you are expected to achieve in your job, in which case you must ask for a clear job description from which to work.

In summary, consider what the problem is and act – if you don't you will never fulfil your own potential and you may never really enjoy work.

stress – the ultimate de-motivator

When people are unhappy at work they can become stressed, and stress can lead to illness. Listed below are some of the causes of stress at work.

1 *Too much work* This can mean that you have too much work to do in too little time, or that because your job is complicated you are always on the edge of losing control of what's going on. One remedy for this is to look at *time management techniques* which help us to use time effectively. Another remedy is to *delegate* to someone else. Remember, delegating does not mean that you are inadequate; the ability to delegate becomes more and more important as we rise higher in an organisation.

2 *Bad relationships with your boss or colleagues* We need to look closely and honestly at what it is that causes bad relationships.
- Is it me or them at the root of the problem?
- Can I talk to my boss about it?

Often bad relationships are caused by simple misunderstandings about who does what, or who takes responsibility for what. In these cases it is essential to bring the problem into the open. (See the section 'Assertiveness' in chapter 4 for hints on how to do this.)

3 *Lack of autonomy* This is about feeling that you have no control over what happens at work – you are constantly having to get permission to do things and have no say in the decision-making process. This might be because you have a low-level job in the organisation, but now you are ready for promotion; or it might be because you have a boss who refuses to delegate or let control out of his hands. If the job is a problem, a talk to personnel about your chances of promotion may help; if this has no effect, then you may need to move jobs. If the boss is the problem then things are more tricky – talking to him or her might help, and it's certainly worth a try. If this has no effect, then again it may be time to move on to a position where your talents will be appreciated.

4 *Role ambiguity* When we are not clear about quite what is expected of us, we experience role ambiguity. The remedy is to seek clarification. Talk to your boss – don't get emotional, just explain clearly how you feel and the problems that arise from the situation. Again, it is worth reading through your job description as well.

5 *Role conflict* Various kinds of role conflict can occur, for example when you have conflicting demands from your boss and your colleagues. Another, which often affects women in particular, is the conflict between work roles and home roles; for example, a mother with a sick child is torn between staying at home with the child and going to work. Role conflict can be difficult to resolve, but that shouldn't prevent us from seeking solutions and discussing the problem with those concerned; it may help to take the pressure off.

6 *Sexual harassment* A problem which is increasingly coming out into the open is that of sexual harassment at work; that is, unwanted/uninvited sexual advances. Tysoe (1988: 40–41) recommends the following:

'The best technique at a personal level appears to be to assert yourself and to make very clear what you find offensive. Do it in a joking fashion if you have to, but make sure they understand you mean it . . . With co-workers . . . if joking doesn't work the best plan is probably to express your feelings plainly. With your boss, if you can't face doing that directly try the "I never mix business with pleasure, I find it impossible to be taken seriously as a fellow worker otherwise, it would ruin our working relationship" type of tactics. One recommended strategy is to write the harasser a letter, with exact dates and places for everything that's happened (keeping a diary of events can be useful if it comes to a confrontation). Say how you feel about it, and what you want to happen. Keep a copy in case you need to take matters further.'

If things get too bad, see if you can find other victims, and complain and/or go to your union for advice. The important thing is to speak out. Don't feel embarrassed about it, because you will not only be helping yourself but also others who may be suffering from this problem too but are afraid to say so.

Stress comes out in a number of ways such as insomnia, headaches, tiredness, lack of concentration, inability to cope, smoking heavily, drinking heavily and general feelings of dissatisfaction. It is important to try to determine what is causing the stress, and to act to stop it.

GROUP DISCUSSION

Form into groups of three or four people. Each participant must think of a stressful situation that he or she has encountered. Discuss each situation as a group, and consider:
* *why the situation was stressful*
* *what strategy could have been adopted to improve the situation.*

---

feeling a failure

Psychologists have found that people differ in something called 'locus of control', which refers to whether we think that things happen as a result of our own efforts (internal locus of control), or are a result of other factors (external locus of control). Rotter (1966) designed a questionnaire to measure this, using statements like 'Becoming a success is a matter of hard work, luck has little or nothing to do with it' (agreement with this indicates an internal locus of control), or 'Getting a good job depends mainly on being in the right place at the right time' (agreement indicates an external locus of control).

Most of us are prone to the self-serving bias, which means that we tend to say that our successes are due to our own efforts and our failures are due to circumstances beyond our control. For example, when a salesman makes a good sale he will put it down to his wonderful sales technique and his irresistible powers of persuasion, but if he fails to make the sale he will put it down to things like the prospect was impossible to do business with, or the secretary made an appointment with the wrong person. This bias serves to protect us and our ego from getting too dented.

However, there are some people who are *not* prone to the self-serving bias and they regard success as being due to external factors, and failures as being entirely their own fault. If you are one of these people, you are likely to say, 'It's no good, there's no point in trying, I just can't succeed, I failed because I'm hopeless so there's no point in going through that again.' But if you try to think positively about yourself you *can* break out of this depressing outlook. One good way to start is to set your sights low – maybe you just try to do very difficult things. First, do something you *know* you can achieve, and when you do achieve it make sure you remind yourself that you got there because *you wanted to*. Start thinking about your failures and realise that almost all of them, if not *all* of them, were in fact not your fault. Think back over the situations, and you will probably find that there were other factors involved. If not, then did you really give it your best shot, or did you give up too easily?

Studies have shown that we can learn to feel helpless. That is, we learn that doing anything will be ineffective, so we do nothing. But often the circumstances in which we learned that we were ineffective were in fact such that no-one could have succeeded in them; hence our feeling of being a failure is quite inappropriate. Think about it. Most of us can succeed at something. Often it's only a matter of finding out what it is we are good at.

summary

- ▶ Motivation refers to the force of energy that directs and propels us into action.
- ▶ Motivation at work is especially important in recruitment, management and self-motivation.
- ▶ When recruiting, needs theories are useful for matching the job to the applicant.
- ▶ Maslow believed that needs form a hierarchy and that we move up the hierarchy in an ordered way.
- ▶ Psychologists have also studied the need for achievement, the need for affiliation and the need for power.

- In management, reinforcement, equity theory, Herzberg's motivation–hygiene theory and expectancy theory can be useful.
- Stress can be a serious factor in de-motivation.
- Feeling a failure can be caused by inappropriate attributions of success and failure.

suggestions for further reading

Cooper, C. L. and **Makin, P.** (eds) (1984) *Psychology for Managers*, British Psychological Society and Macmillan, London. See chapter 5, 'Motivation at work' and chapter 14, 'Stress'.

Feldman, D. C. and **Arnold, H. J.** (1983) *Managing Individual and Group Behaviour in Organizations*, McGraw-Hill. A detailed discussion of motivation in organisations covering the main theories and how to design reward systems.

Hunt, J. (1982) *Managing People at Work*, Pan Books Ltd, London. Covers many aspects of managing at work. The first two chapters particularly concentrate on motivation and needs theories. Quite easy to read.

4. *leadership*

In this chapter we explore how theorists have approached the question of leadership and how to identify your own leadership qualities in terms of some of these theories. Then we look at the skills needed to be an effective leader.

It will soon become apparent that there are many ideas about why leaders are effective and how they get results. It will also be clear that although there are 'born leaders', no-one can really say what it is that makes these people special. However, we can identify certain skills that will help you to lead.

general principles

At work, most tasks are carried out in groups. Social groups usually develop some kind of hierarchy, and if no formal leader is appointed it is often the case that two leaders will emerge:

1 *The task leader*, who takes decisions about how the work is to be carried out.

2 *The socio-emotional leader*, who will look after the welfare of the group members.

However, in a work context there is usually only one leader and he is expected to take on both these responsibilities.

Essentially, leadership means that one person (the leader) is consciously trying to get other people (the followers) to do something the leader wants them to do. So the study of leadership is all about trying to understand how the leader comes to have influence over the followers. What is it that will result in some leaders being seen as effective?

leadership is a two-way process

One thing that makes leadership such a difficult thing to study is that leadership is not a one-way process; leaders do not just issue orders which are unfailingly carried out by their faithful followers. Although leaders can and do influence their followers, followers can also influence leaders. Indeed, the nature of the followers is quite important.

A study by Lowin and Craig (1968) showed this rather clearly. They set up an organisation and then set about hiring people to supervise the work of a group of secretaries. Unknown to their new bosses, the secretaries were working with the experimenters. One group of secretaries had been told to work efficiently, and the other group were to be inefficient. Lowin and Craig found that the behaviour of the secretaries made a considerable difference to the behaviour of their bosses. The bosses in charge of the inefficient secretaries supervised their work more closely, reminded them of their mistakes more often, criticised the amount of time the secretaries spent on breaks, and spent more time checking up on their whereabouts and what they were doing. They also became more directive, less considerate and less friendly towards their secretaries than the bosses who were in charge of the efficient secretaries. From this we can see that leaders are affected by the behaviour of their followers quite strongly. The practical implication of this is that leaders need to take into account the context in which they are operating when formulating their strategy, and adopt the optimal style for achieving their objectives.

the theories

trait theory

The basic assumption of trait theory is that there are certain personality traits that differentiate a good leader from the rest.

This approach stems from the idea of the charismatic leader, such as Napoleon, Churchill, Hitler, and so on. Great leaders should have certain identifiable characteristics that we can learn from in order to succeed as leaders ourselves.

Research into this approach was carried out in the first half of the century, and the whole area was reviewed in 1948 by Stogdill who concluded that 'a person does not become a leader by virtue of the possession of some combination of traits'. He went on to say that 'the pattern of personal characteristics of the leader must bear some relevant relationship to the characteristics, activities and goals of the followers'.

The publication of this conclusion led to great disillusionment with this type of research and theoretical approach. However, the outcome was that researchers concentrated on what made some leaders effective and others ineffective, with a view to developing a testing procedure to screen for who might make an effective manager in an organisational setting (Feldman and Arnold, 1983). There are presently several tests available for assessing leadership, management potential and management style.

In 1974 Stogdill carried out another review of the leadership literature during the period 1949–74, again examining studies which had concentrated on the trait approach, and he found evidence to show that certain personality traits, abilities and social skills were commonly possessed by good leaders (Table 2).

PRACTICAL EXERCISE

Form into groups of three. Each group needs paper and a pen or pencil. Name two well-known leaders each, and using the characteristics listed in Table 2, see how many of these are possessed by the leaders you have listed. Are there other characteristics which your leaders possess that are not shown in Table 2? Which do you think are the most important characteristics?

Feldman and Arnold concluded that 'while a focus on leadership traits alone cannot explain all we need to know regarding effective leadership in organisations, leadership traits are also far from irrelevant to such an understanding. A balanced and complete understanding of leadership effectiveness in organisations must take into account the personal traits and skills of the leaders'.

Clearly then not all of us are destined to be leaders. It seems that there are some characteristics we need to have to begin with, but many of the traits listed can be learnt, so do not despair if you are not a 'born leader'. (See, for example, the section, 'Assertiveness', on pages 59–63.) Self-confidence can be enhanced; it can come from a sense of self-worth.

Table 2 *Characteristics of a good leader*

Personality traits
> Adaptability
> Adjustment (normality)
> Aggressiveness and assertiveness
> Dominance
> Emotional balance and control
> Independence (nonconformity)
> Originality and creativity
> Personal integrity (ethical conduct)
> Self-confidence

Abilities
> Intelligence
> Judgement and decisiveness
> Knowledge
> Fluency of speech

Social skills
> Ability to enlist cooperation
> Administrative ability
> Cooperativeness
> Popularity and prestige
> Sociability
> Social participation
> Tact and diplomacy

Adapted from Feldman and Arnold, 1983

GROUP DISCUSSION

Reconsider the list in Table 2. Discuss whether you believe the characteristics named can be learnt or whether they are inborn and unchangeable. If they can be learnt, can you make suggestions as to how to develop them?

Fiedler's contingency theory

This theory is based on the idea that a leader's effectiveness is *contingent* on the degree of compatibility between the leader's approach and the situation in which he is trying to lead.

Fiedler (1967) suggested that there are basically two types of leader: those whose main concern is doing a good job – that is, they are concerned with carrying out the task effectively (task-oriented) – and those whose main concern is with developing good interpersonal relationships (people-oriented). This division between task-oriented and people-oriented leaders is also put forward by other theorists and will be discussed in more detail.

Fiedler argued that *situations* can be classified by the extent to which they are favourable to leaders. There are three factors. The most important factor is the relationship between the leader and his followers – the better the relationship the more favourable the situation is for the leader. The second most important factor is how structured the task at hand is – the more structured it is the more favourable the situation is for the leader because he or she can more easily monitor what the followers are doing. The least important factor is called position power – this means the amount of power that the leader has from his or her position in the organisation. For example, a director has more position power than a filing clerk. The more position power the leader has, the more favourable the situation is to him or her.

According to this theory, leaders who are people-oriented are most effective when situations are moderately favourable, but are less effective in highly favourable and highly unfavourable situations. Leaders who are task-oriented do better in situations which are highly favourable or are highly unfavourable.

A basic assumption of the theory is that personality cannot be changed; therefore if you find yourself in the 'wrong' kind of situation you will not be an effective leader. So if anything has to change it is the situation and not the leader.

Evidence for this theory is mixed, but the important contribution from it is to try and actually specify exactly what it is that makes some leaders effective and others not effective, by classifying situations as well as taking account of leader characteristics. Thus you cannot expect to always succeed as a leader just because you seem to have all the requisite personal qualities; you must also take into account the situation you find yourself in.

the Vroom and Yetton model

This approach is rather different to the previous two. It is not strictly speaking a theory about leadership, but is a model of how leaders *should* behave, based on previous research.

Whereas Fiedler's theory suggests that leaders have a certain set of characteristics (person-oriented or task-oriented), and that these will determine how effective the leader will be according to the situation, Vroom and Yetton's model is based on the idea that leaders *are* adaptable and that they should analyse the situation and adopt the appropriate behaviour for it. So they concentrate on context, assuming that leaders are able to analyse the situation in which they are working and dispassionately choose a suitable course of action.

Vroom and Yetton's model concentrates on how much the leader should allow subordinates to participate in the decision-making process. They believe that the degree of participation enjoyed by subordinates should vary according to the situation in which the decision is to be made.

Table 3 shows the five different alternatives between which the leader can choose.

Table 3 *The five decision styles in the Vroom–Yetton model of leadership*

A = autocratic   **C** = consultative   **G** = group

AI   You solve the problem or make the decision yourself using the information available to you at the present time.

AII   You obtain any necessary information from subordinates, then decide on a solution to the problem yourself. You may or may not tell subordinates the purpose of your questions or give information about the problem or decision you are working on. The input provided by them is clearly in response to your request for specific information. They do not play a role in the definition of the problem or in generating or evaluating alternative solutions.

CI   You share the problem with the relevant subordinates individually, getting their ideas and suggestions without bringing them together as a group. Then you make the decision. This decision may or may not reflect your subordinates' influence.

CII   You share the problem with your subordinates in a group meeting. In this meeting you obtain their ideas and suggestions. Then you make the decision, which may or may not reflect your subordinates' influence.

GII   You share the problem with your subordinates as a group. Together you generate and evaluate alternatives and attempt to reach agreement (consensus) on a solution. Your role is much like that of chairman, coordinating the discussion, keeping it focused on the problem, and making sure that the critical issues are discussed. You can provide the group with information or ideas that you have but you do not try to 'press' them to adopt 'your' solution and are willing to accept and implement any solution that has the support of the entire group.

From Vroom and Jago, 1978

When a decision has to be made you need to choose which approach to take. Vroom and Yetton give seven rules to follow in order to choose your decision-making style. These are divided into those that protect the quality of the decision and those that protect the acceptance of the decision.

Rules that protect the quality of the decision

1 *The leader information rule* If the quality of the decision is important and the leader does not possess enough information or expertise to solve the problem by him or herself, then eliminate AI.

2 *The goal congruence rule* If the quality of the decision is important and subordinates are not likely to pursue the organisational goals in their efforts to solve this problem, then eliminate GII.

3 *The unstructured problem rule* If the quality of the decision is important and the leader lacks the necessary information or know-how to solve the problem by him or herself, and if the problem is unstructured, then the method of problem-solving should involve a group of subordinates who will possess the relevant information. Therefore eliminate AI, AII and CI.

Rules that protect the acceptance of the decision

4 *The acceptance rule* If the acceptance of the decision by subordinates is important/crucial to implementation, and an autocratic approach is not acceptable, then eliminate AI and AII.

5 *The conflict rule* If acceptance of the decision by subordinates is important/crucial to implementation and an autocratic approach is not acceptable, and disagreement amongst subordinates is likely, then an approach should be used which can enable disagreements to be discussed and resolved. Eliminate AI, AII and CI, which do not allow discussion.

6 *The fairness rule* If the quality of the decision is not important, but acceptance by subordinates is (and if an autocratic approach is unlikely to be accepted), then eliminate AI, AII, CI and CII; that is, you have to use G.

7 *The acceptance priority rule* If acceptance of the decision is critical, but may not happen if an autocratic approach is taken, and if subordinates are motivated to pursue organisational goals, then methods which give equal partnership in the decision-making process can provide greater acceptance and do not risk the quality of the decision. Therefore, eliminate AI, AII, CI and CII; that is, you have to use G.

After you have been through the seven rules, you will be left with what Vroom and Yetton call the 'feasible set' of decision-making approaches. If this feasible set still has more than one approach left, then the leader can choose whichever he prefers. For example, he may choose the one that is quickest to implement (AI).

This approach is important and popular with managers because once mastered it is easy to use and research shows that it can be successful in practice.

PRACTICAL EXERCISE
Using the Vroom and Yetton model to make decisions

Read the following description carefully. After reading it, use the Vroom and Yetton model to choose which decision-making style you should adopt.

You are the manufacturing manager in a large electronics plant. The company's management has always been searching for ways of increasing efficiency. They have recently installed new machines and put in a new simplified work system, but to the surprise of everyone, including yourself, the expected increase in productivity has not been realised. In fact, production has begun to drop, quality has fallen off, and the number of employee separations has risen.

You do not believe that there is anything wrong with the machines. You have had reports from other companies who are using them and they confirm this opinion. You have also had representatives from the firm that built the machines to look over them and they report that they are operating at peak efficiency.

You suspect that some parts of the new work system may be responsible for the change, but this view is not widely shared among your immediate subordinates, who are four first-line supervisors, each in charge of a section, and your supply manager. The drop in production has been variously attributed to poor training of the operators, lack of an adequate system of financial incentives, and poor morale. Clearly, this is an issue about which there is considerable depth of feeling within individuals and potential disagreement among your subordinates.

This morning you received a phone call from your division manager. He had just received your production figures for the last six months and was calling to express his concern. He indicated that the problem was yours to solve in any way that you think best, but that he would like to know within a week what steps you plan to take.

You share your division manager's concern with the falling productivity and know that your men are also concerned. The problem is to decide what steps to take to rectify the situation.

From V. H. Vroom 'A new look at managerial decision making', in *Organizational Dynamics*, Spring 1973, New York: AMACOM, a division of American Management Associations, 1973, p. 72

GROUP DISCUSSION
(See end of chapter for the correct solution.)

Do you believe, having used it, that Vroom and Yetton's model can be useful to managers in situations such as that described here? Can you think of situations in which the model would not be useful?

path goal theory

This is a highly complex theory and we won't go into great detail here. However, it is interesting because it discusses different leadership *styles*. Also, it assumes that a leader can adopt any of these styles at will.

It is called *path goal theory* because it depends upon the idea that leaders must set attainable goals and make it clear to followers how they can attain these goals (the *path*) – which is pretty reasonable when you think about it! The result of doing this should be to increase subordinates' job satisfaction and motivation levels by making it clear to them how their performance on the job can lead to positive outcomes or rewards. Hence the link between the amount of effort put in and subsequent performance is made clear by the leader. This means that people can feel they have positively accomplished something. The leadership styles are used according to the situation in which the leader finds him or herself.

There are four distinct leadership styles:

1 *Directive leadership* This style involves very clear directives to followers – they will be told who does what, how, when and where. It is a strong style of leadership with strong rules and procedures which must be followed. This style is effective when followers see themselves as being low in ability; then they can leave the problems/responsibilities to the leader. It is also effective when the task is ambiguous, because the leader can clarify what needs to be done.

2 *Supportive leadership* This style is rather like being a socio-emotional leader. The leader is friendly and relaxed and tends to treat followers as equals, and tries to make work an enjoyable experience. This style is effective when followers are high in ability and highly motivated. When the task to be accomplished is stressful, dissatisfying or frustrating, this style can lead to increased job satisfaction.

3 *Participative leadership* This style of leadership is characterised by shared decision-making – the followers participate in the leader's running of the group. Again this is effective when followers are high in ability and highly motivated. Sometimes though this style can be seen as weak.

4 *Achievement-oriented leadership* This is a style which lays emphasis on achievement and excellence. Such a leader encourages followers to achieve challenging goals and to take personal responsibility for fulfilling them. Subordinates with a high need for achievement (see chapter 3) will respond well to this style.

Overall, this theory has helped managers to look at how their leadership style is flexible and should be modified according to the demands of the situation.

the managerial grid

The last theory we look at concentrates on leadership style in terms of whether the leader/manager is task-oriented or people-oriented. The theory uses a grid onto which managers are placed and described in terms of these qualities.

If you want to determine your own managerial style, turn to Appendix 1, which gives you full information on how to do so.

Blake and Mouton developed this approach, which takes into account that leaders have to take care of both the task and the group. They classify managers in terms of what they call *the managerial grid* (Table 4).

Table 4 *The managerial grid*

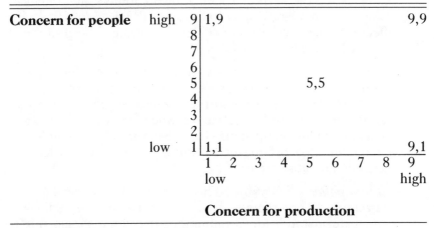

Adapted from Blake and Mouton, 1978

Blake and Mouton identify five main managerial styles.

1,9 *Country club management* This style of manager has a high concern for people, and values relationships more than productivity. This means that there is a comfortable, friendly organisation atmosphere and work tempo.

1,1 *Impoverished management* This style of manager has little concern for people or for production. The manager aims to keep his or her job and to keep out of trouble and exerts the minimum amount of effort required to stay in the organisation.

5,5 *Organisation man management* This is a compromise position aiming to produce as much as possible and keep people happy. Thus adequate organisation performance is possible through balancing the necessity to produce work with maintaining morale of people at a satisfactory level.

9,1 *Authority–obedience* Here the manager concentrates on production and ignores people. Thus efficiency in operations results from arranging conditions of work in such a way that human elements interfere to a minimum degree.

9,9 *Team management* The manager attains high levels of production by gaining commitment and harnessing group and individual motivations to the task. Thus work accomplishment is from committed people; interdependence is through a common stake in organisation purpose, which leads to relationships of trust and respect.

Blake and Mouton argue that 9,9 is the best style for a manager, although a leader should be able to vary style according to the needs of the situation. They suggest five conditions which need to be considered when adopting a managerial style. Which managerial style is dominant for any given person in any particular situation is influenced by any one or several sets of conditions.

1 *Organisation* The manager's behaviour is often influenced by the organisational culture within which he or she works, so the manager may choose 'the right way to manage' according to organisational norms. Hence the style adopted may reflect little of the manager's personal style if the organisation does not allow for individual flexibility.

2 *Situation* The style adopted during a crisis is likely to be very different from that which is adopted when things are running smoothly. It may well be appropriate to adopt a task-oriented approach when the team is under pressure to complete a task quickly.

3 *Values* The manager may have strongly-held beliefs about how people should be managed or about the way to manage to get results.

4 *Personality* The dominant managerial style may result from deep-seated personality differences.

5 *Chance* A person may adopt a particular style because he or she does not realise that there are other options available. Perhaps the manager has not had the opportunity to learn other styles.

If you have not yet tried classifying yourself using the grid (Table 4), you should do so now. By becoming aware of your style and how it evolved, Blake and Mouton believe that you can optimise your performance. They recognise the importance of situational variables, e.g. organisational culture and task – (1) and (2) above – but emphasise managerial flexibility. They do, however, believe that 9,9 is the 'best' style.

One problem with this approach is the way that the styles are measured – the questions to be answered are rather simple and not reliable in the sense that the answer today may be different from the answer given tomorrow. The second problem with the approach is that really it just adds to the confusion of theories about leadership; the individual is put into a category – so what? Reddin (1970) has developed this approach even further and has a matrix of styles, which may be helpful as a means of helping managers to think about their approach to managing. Certainly the two dimensions are valid and recur in many approaches to leadership or management, but research on these dimensions has produced mixed results. However, the following are established:

- When the work group is under pressure to produce, then a task-oriented style of leadership will be more effective.
- When the work group is small, a person-oriented style is more effective than a task-oriented style if the group members are to be satisifed.
- When subordinates' needs are mainly concerned with security and structure, then they prefer a task-oriented leader.
- When employees have a low need for structure, then a person-oriented approach is more effective.

leadership in practice

The theories described above are interesting and useful because they help to make us aware of the range of styles available to us as potentially good leaders, but they do seem rather abstract. The guidelines they give are too general. After all, the main task of a manager is to get employees to perform to the best of their ability. As all managers know, this is much easier to talk about than to accomplish.

sources of power

How does the leader gain the power needed to control and influence subordinates? Five sources of power for a leader in an organisation have been identified. Some derive from the *leader's personality*, others derive from the *leader's role* in the organisation. The most effective leaders are likely to have access to all five power sources.

1 *Reward power*   If the leader has control over rewards that are valued by followers, then the leader's power will increase. From a personal point of view this might mean praise or attention from the leader; from an organisational point of view this might mean

promotion, pay rises, or perks such as company cars and business lunches.

2 *Coercive power* This is the opposite of reward power and means the punishments that are available to the leader. Again they can be divided into personal punishments such as criticism, and organisational punishments such as not promoting followers who misbehave, or not authorising pay rises.

3 *Legitimate/position power* This is power derived from the leader's role in the organisation, and has nothing to do with personal characteristics. For example, employees are likely to regard it as quite legitimate for the managing director to demand all the files on a certain subject to be delivered to his or her office first thing in the morning, but not for the director's secretary to do so without authorisation.

4 *Expert power* This is power derived entirely from the leader's personal abilities/expertise and has nothing to do with the leader's organisational role. If followers are able to see their leader as an expert on the task they are doing, they will respect the leader's judgement and follow his or her direction much more readily than if they do not think the leader is an expert.

5 *Referent power* This again is entirely dependent on the leader's personal characteristics and not on the leader's organisational role. It is about how much followers refer to their leader as a model, how much they look up to the leader and want to be like him or her. The more they do this, the more referent power we can say that the leader has.

Even if a leader has access to all these sources of power, it does not mean that he or she will be an effective leader. That depends on how the leader decides to use power; that is, on what it is he or she influences subordinates to do.

assertiveness

So you want to be a leader, a captain of industry, maybe just manager of your department? But you can't say no – you are a human doormat. Don't despair, help is at hand. Or perhaps you find that you most certainly can say no, but . . . people are always accusing you of being aggressive/macho/a raving feminist? Don't worry, you too can be helped. What's the answer? *Assertiveness*.

Assertiveness training is fast becoming a very popular form of management training, especially in the USA, and here in the UK its popularity is growing rapidly. Why? Because it works. People attending such courses find they derive personal benefits from them.

Assertiveness was originally taught to people who had problems in standing up for their rights. Lange and Jakubowski (1976) defined it as involving '. . . standing up for personal rights and expressing thoughts, feelings and beliefs in direct, honest and appropriate ways which respect the rights of other people.' Alberti and Emmons (1975) say that assertion is behaviour which '. . . enables a person to act in his or her own best interests, to stand up for herself or himself without undue anxiety, to express honest feelings comfortably, or to exercise personal rights without denying the rights of others.' People who are skilled in assertiveness are easy to work with because there is no 'secret agenda' – they say what they think and feel clearly and openly, so a lot of time is saved all round.

Assertiveness is not the same as aggressiveness. Assertiveness means standing up for yourself without attacking the other person, whereas aggressiveness usually does mean some kind of attack on the other person, either verbal or physical.

Psychologists usually describe three types of response: aggressive, assertive and passive. Imagine a situation where the boss tells you that the Christmas lunch that you spent so long agonising over was a total shambles:

BOSS That Christmas lunch you organised was a total mess. Whatever got into you putting Eileen next to Fred and forgetting that my secretary's a vegetarian?

PASSIVE Oh, yes, I'm dreadfully sorry, I, er, just don't know what happened, everything just got . . . er . . . out of hand . . .

AGGRESSIVE Well, what did you expect? That fool Eileen just barged in and the b..... restaurant didn't get their act together. You can stuff your Christmas lunch up your turkey.

ASSERTIVE I see what you mean. However, Eileen refused to be seated anywhere else, and the restaurant made an unfortunate mistake with the vegetarian meal. Still, Fred did come up to me later and say that he felt he had been too hasty in his judgement of Eileen and that now they are becoming quite friendly.

Some writers also distinguish between direct and indirect aggression. Indirect aggression covers things like sulking when you don't get your way, or stomping around the office and slamming doors but refusing to discuss what the problem is. Imagine the different responses to someone smoking in a no smoking area:

AGGRESSIVE   'Hey, you, clear off! This is a no smoking area. Put out or get out!'

INDIRECTLY AGGRESSIVE   Waves hands about in the air towards the smoker as if to fan the smoke away. Coughs loudly.

PASSIVE   Doesn't say anything and hopes someone else will.

ASSERTIVE   'Excuse me, do you realise that this is a no smoking area? Cigarette smoke affects me quite badly, so I'd be grateful if you wouldn't smoke here.'

Assertiveness skills

1 *Basic assertion*   This is simply standing up for your rights. Hargie (1986) gives the example of being interrupted when speaking – you say, 'Excuse me, I would like to finish what I was saying.'

2 *Empathic assertion*   You empathise with the other person's feelings before making your assertion. So you might say, 'I understand your reservations about this new working practice, Pete, but I must insist that you stick with it until the management meeting on Thursday.'

3 *Escalating assertion*   This is used when, after an assertive response, the other person is not to be turned down. Imagine a salesman who won't give up:

A 'No thank you, I do not want to buy any of your carbon paper.'
B 'I've already told you that I don't wish to purchase any of your products.'
C 'I've told you twice that I do not want to buy any of your products. Please leave now.'

4 *Confronting assertion*   Used when someone says he or she will do something but doesn't. The asserter spells out the problem clearly: 'Pete, you told me that this report would be on my desk this afternoon. It is not on my desk. Please go and finish writing it now so that I can take it home to read tonight.'

Assertiveness has to be used appropriately, of course, and the situation is an important factor in how effective it will be. Some people find it easier to be assertive in some situations than in others, for example at home but not at work. The country in which you find yourself can be important too – Furnham (1979) pointed out that assertiveness may not be appropriate in countries that value humility or subservience.

Women may also find it more difficult to be assertive because there is a popular stereotype of women being more submissive and passive than men, which can be difficult to overcome. Research has shown that reactions to female assertiveness depend on the attitude of the responder. People who value women make no distinction between an assertive male or a female, but people who do not value women tend to take a poor opinion of assertive women. So it may pay for a woman to temper her assertiveness in the company of chauvinistic types!

We also know that assertive people react positively to assertion by others, but passive people react negatively. So we should take the other person's nature into account when deciding whether or not to be assertive.

Reactions to assertiveness

What will happen when you are suddenly transformed into a new, assertive person? Well, be prepared for some surprises; studies have shown that people certainly do react to the newly assertive individual. First, you may get the 'back-biting' response; that is, comments made loudly behind your back such as, 'Who does he think he is all of a sudden?' Secondly, you may encounter aggression when people start to feel that you might be getting the upper hand. Thirdly, meek people might go over the top and respond by apologising profusely. (You might suggest to them that they too look into developing skills in assertiveness!) Fourthly, you may encounter concealed aggression – outwardly people respond well, but secretly they harbour resentment at your new-found confidence.

Overall, though, the benefits will outweigh the drawbacks and people will settle down to accept the new you.

When not to be assertive

There are times when assertiveness just is not appropriate. There are at least three such contexts.

1 When someone is in a difficult situation, and not deliberately denying your personal rights. For example, the new switchboard operator may not mean to keep you waiting to make that important outside call; perhaps she is just overwhelmed by the new and complex switchboard. Here you would simply be putting her under pressure if you insisted on making a fuss, and

you would be better advised to overlook it until she has had a chance to settle into the job.

2 When the person you are dealing with is a very sensitive soul. Some people will react by bursting into tears or by becoming extraordinarily aggressive. Nothing you can do will change the way they react, so it is best here to be non-assertive.

3 Manipulating others. Be sensible – sometimes you need to get what you want by cunning! For example, when the police stop you it is better to go for the passive, apologetic approach!

Assertiveness will help you to say no when you want to without feeling guilty about it. It will help to improve your communication with others since you will be able to state what you want and how you feel. Finally, developing assertiveness skills will improve your self-confidence and leadership skills.

PRACTICAL EXERCISE – Being assertive

This exercise is designed to give you practice in two types of assertive behaviour – standing up for your rights, and saying no. These are often identified as being difficult to accomplish.

You need a partner for this exercise. Decide on one situation in which you find it difficult to stand up for yourself, e.g. telling someone they have not carried out the job properly, taking an article back to a shop because there is something wrong with it. Select another situation in which you find it hard to say no, e.g. when someone asks you to do them a favour which is unreasonable.

Role-play the first situation, in which you find it hard to stand up for yourself. Discuss afterwards what you found difficult. How did you cope? Work with a partner, to give and get feedback on tone of voice (too timid? too strident?) and non-verbal behaviour (did you avoid eye contact?).

Role-play the situation in which you are to practise saying no. Remember, if the request is unreasonable you must avoid making excuses about why you can't comply. Learn to turn such requests down firmly but politely. Reverse roles. Discuss afterwards how it felt to say no. Did you succeed?

---

leading groups

Assertiveness is essentially a one-to-one skill. Now we look at some of the skills that are needed to lead groups, since many tasks at work are carried out in this context.

Focus on the task

One of the most important functions of the leader is to keep the group focused on the task in hand. This is especially true in the context of meetings. The leader needs to establish early on the aim or aims of the group, and suggest ways in which they can be accomplished.

Clarify what is happening

The group leader needs to clear up any confusion, keep the group to the point, and point out alternatives. It is always useful to paraphrase group members' contributions to the discussion to make sure that everyone has really understood what each member is saying. It is also useful to *summarise* periodically – this orients the group to where they are going, what has been said and what still needs to be done.

Ask questions

To encourage full contributions it is useful if the leader asks questions – to get more information, to invite opinions and to help generate ideas.

Problems with participants

There are people who just won't talk in group meetings. One way to overcome this is for the leader to warn the group that he or she will be asking for contributions from all of the group members; this avoids singling out any one person. Also, the group should be allowed to experience periods of silence. Someone will eventually contribute if the group isn't feeling too pressured. Sometimes provocative questions will encourage participation.

The opposite problem is the person who will not shut up. This can be very trying. One approach is for the leader to say something like, 'Pete, if we aren't careful this is going to turn into a two-way conversation.' It is important not to stamp on these people – often just a gentle reminder will work wonders. After all, they are probably participating for the best of reasons.

Reducing group tension

Sometimes some members of the group will feel very strongly about something and may have strongly conflicting views which they cannot resolve. One way of getting over this is for the leader to place the emphasis on the issue and not on the personalities involved, to bring the whole thing into a wider context. Another approach is to introduce humour to defuse the situation. Often humour allows the warring parties to back down without loss of face, and can act as a cue that things have gone far enough.

leadership style and group performance

Lewin, Lippett and White (1939) carried out a classic study on how leadership style affected the performance of groups of 10-year-old boys who belonged to an after-school boys' club. The boys were split into three groups, each led with a different style:

1 *Autocratic* The leader told the boys what models to make and who to work with. He would sometimes blame or praise the boys but offered no supporting explanations of this.

2 *Democratic* The leader discussed the possibilities for projects and teams and allowed the boys to make their own decisions. He would praise or blame the boys and offer explanations, e.g. 'It's very good the way you have managed to make your plane more realistic by adding windows.'

3 *Laissez-faire* The boys were left to their own devices. The leader only gave help when asked to, which didn't happen often, and offered no praise or blame.

What the study showed was that under the autocratic leader the boys became either aggressive towards each other or just apathetic. They were submissive in their approaches to the leader. If the leader left the room, the boys became disruptive and stopped working. If frustrated by a problem the boys would blame each other rather than cooperate to solve it. Under the democratic leader, relationships between the boys were better, they showed less aggression, and they liked each other more. Approaches to the leader were usually task-related. Although slightly less work was done than with the autocratic leader, the boys did not stop work when the leader left the room, and when a problem arose the boys would cooperate to solve it. Under the laissez-faire leader the groups were chaotic. The boys' relationships were aggressive and very little work was done whether the leader was there or not. These groups did not even do enough work to encounter problems related to the task; they just gave up when the work became at all difficult or demanding.

Therefore, by giving explanations and encouraging participative decision-making, the democratic leader achieved the best results. As Feldman and Arnold (1983) say, 'Individuals under democratic leadership were more satisfied, had higher morale, were more creative, and had better relationships with their superiors.' Other studies have supported this finding. The democratic leader also used rewards like praise to encourage his boys.

However, one thing that we must not lose sight of is that leaders can and do adjust their behaviour to suit the situation in which they are working. Also, any one kind of leadership style is unlikely to be effective across all kinds of situation.

The work implication of such findings is that managers are likely to find that a democratic approach will stimulate good working practice in a steady way, without the need for constant supervision. But flexibility is important for successful leadership.

summing it all up

Overall, leadership is a skill. It is certainly important to develop interpersonal skills, a flexible approach and a good understanding of the theories of motivation and leadership so that we can put all these things into practice at work.

See chapter 3 for further useful ideas on leading and motivating others.

summary

- In groups, very often two leaders emerge, the task leader and the socio-emotional leader. At work, leaders usually have to take on both roles.
- Leadership is a two-way process.
- Trait theories concentrate on the personal qualities which go together to make up a good leader.
- Fiedler argued that a leader's effectiveness is contingent on the degree of compatibility between the leader's approach and the situation in which he or she is leading.
- Vroom and Yetton offered a model allowing leaders to choose the level of participation in any situation.
- Path goal theory highlights four distinctive leadership styles: directive, supportive, participative and achievement-oriented.
- The managerial grid classifies leaders by how task- or person-oriented they are.

- ► Leaders have access to different sorts of power depending on their personality and the situation they are in.
- ► Assertiveness is a useful skill for leaders, allowing them to stand up for their position whilst still respecting the rights of others.
- ► Democratic leadership seems to be the most effective style in effective management.

The answer to the problem set earlier on page 54 is GII.

suggestions for further reading

Blake, R. R. and **Mouton, J. S.** (1978) *The New Managerial Grid*, Gulf Publishing Co., Houston, Texas. This is the full version of their grid theory, if you really want to get to grips with it.

Sidney, E., **Brown, M.** and **Argyle, M.** (1973) *Skills With People. A guide for managers*, Hutchinson & Co., London. Readable paperback which covers most of the main points about leadership skills.

5. *intragroup dynamics*

Whenever three or more people get together a group is formed. Groups form for many different reasons – to perform a task, for social reasons, and so on. In this chapter we look at what happens in a group and how being in a group can change people's behaviour.

You may have noticed that you behave differently when other people are with you than you do when you are alone. For example, social psychologists have found that when we are with other people we often work harder than we do when we work alone – this effect is called *social facilitation*. However, performance only improves when the task is a simple one, like pedalling on a bicycle. When the task to be achieved is more complex (e.g. planning or research) the presence of others can be a distraction and lead to poorer performance. Another effect is called *social loafing* where it is found that as the size of the group is increased, each individual puts in less effort. Again this occurs when the task in hand is a simple one. For example, when several people were asked to clap or cheer as loudly as they could, as the size of the group increased each person decreased the amount of sound that he or she made. The nature of the group's activities (or task) can have a bearing on what happens in terms of group dynamics and individual and group performance.

Organisations are made up of groups of people, in departments for example, or in smaller teams of co-workers. Consequently, to be effective at work we need to be aware of group processes and how they can work for and against us when trying to achieve our objectives. Some of these processes can jeopardise good decision-making and lessen working effectiveness in groups; others are beneficial. We need to develop skills in communicating and working within groups. These skills are discussed in this chapter and the next.

general principles

the presence of others

The mere presence of other people is enough to change our behaviour. Social facilitation is a good example of this. Also, we are less inclined to go to the aid of someone in trouble when others are present than when we are alone (*bystander apathy*). This is probably because we look around, see that no-one else is helping and therefore re-define what we think is happening; that is, we think that perhaps things aren't as bad as they look – after all, no one else is doing anything. We may also feel embarrassed. So we can say that groups can define our reality – as soon as other people are there we look to them for guidance on how we should behave, even if we don't talk to them.

A psychologist friend describes how at parties people are always embarrassed to be the first one to help themselves to the food. He takes advantage of this effect by helping himself first!

what is a group?

Feldman and Arnold (1983) define a group as '. . . a collection of two or more people who: (1) interact with each other; (2) perceive themselves to share some common interests or goals; and (3) come together or are brought together to accomplish some work activity.' So a group consists of people who are working together to achieve a common aim and who are aware of this aim. We do not consider social groups here, only work groups.

Honey (1988) suggests that groups and teams are two different entities. He says:

'A group is a collection of individual people who come together to serve some purpose. A group is a lesser thing than a team, which performs at a higher level of cohesion than a mere group needs to . . . A team is a small group (6 to 8 people is a typical size) who co-operate together in such a way that they accomplish more than the sum total of the individuals. The jargon word for this is synergy.'

Groups are often formed of people who are similar in some way, whereas teams are necessarily composed of people who are different.

Whilst a team sounds like a more desirable thing than a group at work, in fact we do not necessarily need teams for routine tasks;

69

groups are quite satisfactory. Teams are especially important when tasks are ambiguous, difficult and non-routine.

Chell (1987) distinguished between 'family' groups and 'special' groups. *Family groups* are permanent with a stable membership and a task function. *Special groups* are those that are formed for a specific purpose or to address a particular problem. It is these special groups, brought together to achieve a particular result, that are often built deliberately into teams. Team building is discussed in chapter 6. First, though, we look at 'family' groups in organisations.

formal and informal groups

Formal groups

Formal groups are groups which come together especially to achieve a particular task, for example an accounts department is created to administer all accounting tasks within an organisation.

Interestingly, the structure of work groups can affect an individual's job satisfaction. In the 1950s, Bavelas investigated how the communication structure of groups might affect the group members. Several structures were identified; these are shown in Fig. 7.

Fig.7 Structures of communication

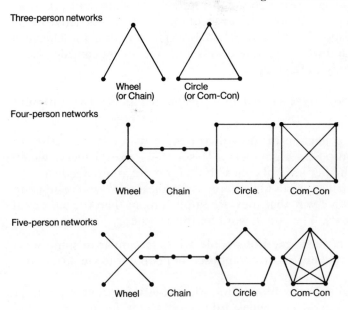

Source: Berkowitz, 1986

Imagine that each dot is a person in the group. The lines represent the lines of communication between them. In the wheel structures (always shown at the left of the diagram) people on the spokes have to communicate through the person located at the hub, and do not communicate directly with each other. In each row, the amount of centralisation decreases from left to right. That is, as centralisation decreases, members can communicate more directly with each other, without needing a central person through whom all messages are routed.

The *com-con* ('completely connected') structure is completely decentralised, allowing any group member to communicate directly with any other.

In centralised structures, individuals on the outlying spokes need the cooperation of the person at the hub to get and give independence to other group members. Research has shown that those on the spokes tend to be dissatisfied with their jobs, because they are dependent on the central position and feel that they lack the freedom for independent action. Conversely, those at the hub tend to be highly satisfied with their job – they are the first to receive any information and thus are able to act on it, giving a high degree of information and autonomy.

When the job at the hub is relatively straightforward – collecting information, relaying messages, answering queries and allocating tasks if necessary, with a simple task to be accomplished – everything works well. Those at the spokes settle down to their job and the person at the hub can increase the efficiency of the group by leaving them free to get on with their work. However, when the task is complex the hub position can become overloaded and can become swamped if there is too much information to handle.

So centralised networks are efficient when the task is fairly simple, whereas the decentralised neworks are better for complex tasks.

Informal groups

Informal groups are not deliberately formed, they evolve naturally. Dalton (1959) identified three kinds of informal group in organisations.

1 *Horizontal cliques* These consist of people all of the same rank or level in the organisation, but not necessarily working together. For example, management trainees may meet at the pub to discuss their progress – they all have something in common.

2 *Vertical cliques*   These are all people who come from the same department, but from different levels within it. For example, the department head, secretary and filing clerk may informally discuss what is happening at work and pass on information to each other when they meet in the lift or the corridors.

3 *Random cliques*   These are made up of people from all parts of the organisation and often form as a way of getting round the rules. For example, a secretary may befriend the people in the postroom so that she can deliver her mail late and still get it franked and sent, even though the rules are that mail must be delivered to the postroom by a certain time.

People usually belong to these informal groups to fulfil some need. The following are the most common:

1 *To accomplish goals*   In the random cliques, by by-passing the system people often find that they can get more done, more easily. They 'work the system' to their advantage – the secretary still manages to get that important letter sent for the boss even though she was late in typing it.

2 *To advance their careers*   By increasing efficiency, e.g. by avoiding red tape or by using an informal network, it is possible to gain a reputation for being the person 'who gets thing done'; or by using informal sources of information it is possible to get the inside story about what promotion may be coming up.

3 *To enhance their reputation*   For example, by being the member of a 'go-ahead' group of management trainees an individual can become known as forward-looking and career-minded.

Being a member of an informal group can be useful in many ways. It always pays to befriend the secretaries in an organisation. They will type work for you when you desperately need to meet deadlines, they always know what is going on – and forewarned is forearmed! The informal group can be a useful source of information. These networks of communication should never be ignored, nor their importance in organisations discounted.

social roles

At work we have a job title. Fulfilling the expectations of the job means taking on the role of that job. Argyle (1988) defines a role as '. . . the pattern of behaviour shared by most occupants of a position and which comes to be expected of them'. Taking on a role is rather like putting on a mask; people relate to us in a role and expect us to behave in a way that is appropriate to that role. It is another aspect of conformity to the group. This time the group can be the whole of society, or the organisation for which we work.

Because of these expectations it can be very difficult to resist conforming to the behaviour of the role. An experiment by Zimbardo (1973) showed how roles can take people over. He set up a fake prison study and recruited volunteers to participate. All the volunteers were screened first to make sure that they were 'normal', and were then assigned to be either guards or prisoners. The experiment was scheduled to last for two weeks, but was stopped after five days because the guards were aggressive and tyrannical, whilst the prisoners became apathetic and servile and started to show severe depression. The roles had swamped the participants' own identities.

There can be problems if your work role conflicts with your personality, for instance if you work in a rigid and authoritarian company, but you are relaxed and democratic in your outlook. Role conflict also arises when you occupy two conflicting roles; this is especially common amongst women. For example, a woman may have the role of mother and of reliable, efficient secretary. The two can come into conflict when the mother wants to stay at home with her sick child, but her boss has an important job for her to do that day at work – does she stay at home or go to work?

Role conflict can lead to a great deal of stress, even illness and reduced productivity. Role ambiguity, where a role is unclear or ill-defined, can have the same sort of effects. If this happens to you, go and see your boss and try to talk it through – it won't go away unless you take action. It may be that you have to give up your job, but in many cases compromises can be found.

group norms

Over time groups develop group norms. Group norms are unspoken rules about what is and what is not acceptable within the group. Norms vary from group to group, but in all groups the norms are extremely important and you break them at your peril.

If you conform to group norms you will receive group rewards such as friendship, support from other group members, respect and recognition. If you break group norms you will soon know it – you may be the target of jokes or snide remarks, or you may be denied group rewards; at worst you will be ostracised from the group altogether.

At work, group norms may concern many aspects of job performance such as cooperation with management, job output, timekeeping and standards of dress. Often in groups of workers in factories there are norms about acceptable levels of output – new group members soon learn not to work too hard and to adopt the pace set by the group; failure to do so can lead to a very unhappy working life.

Salancik and Pfeffer (1978) found that if co-workers kept saying that a job was dull, horrible and undesirable, then the job holder usually came to agree with them.

Norms serve to reduce ambiguity and to give structure to the group. When they go against management goals they can cause problems at work, as in the example above – management may want high productivity whilst workers are not prepared to work at that level of performance. However, norms are also useful to increase productivity. If managers and workers have a good relationship, norms can encourage good performance.

Natural leaders often arise within work groups. Sometimes the leader can create group norms; sometimes he is dominated by them too. Some natural leaders are obviously dominant; others can be quietly spoken, but all the same are highly valued group members who define group norms. These natural leaders become important when group performance is poor. Anyone who can communicate with natural leaders is well on the way to influencing group norms through the leaders.

So the group can increase and/or decrease individual productivity at work. The other group members can serve as a model for new workers who are quickly 'socialised' into their new position in the organisation.

GROUP DISCUSSION

Spend five minutes noting down your own social roles. Then spend another five minutes jotting down all the groups that you belong to. Come together as a group and discuss how your roles have different and (perhaps) contrasting expectations. Move on to think about norms in groups:
- *What are the norms of the groups you belong to?*
- *How do they affect your behaviour?*
- *Do you conform to norms? What happens if you don't?*

group processes

conformity

The pressure to conform is a strong and often irresistible force. The tendency for people to conform in a group has interested psychologists for a long time. In some senses there is nothing wrong with conforming – we do it all the time, and indeed if we do not conform we can find ourselves in trouble. For example, at school the non-conformists are often the troublemakers. When we apply for jobs we are taught how we should write our curriculum vitae, how to dress for interviews, how to behave at work, and so on.

So what's wrong with that? The answer is nothing at all, but if we all conformed all the time, nothing would change. Many highly creative people are non-conformists, such as artists, but we have a special position for such people – we allow them 'eccentricity licence'. That is, we recognise that such people tend to be like this and we allow it because of the nature of their work. Without such people society would be impoverished, and the same thinking can also be applied to work. If everyone at work conformed to such an extent that they were afraid to voice their opinion when it differed from that of the group, then new ideas would never be accepted, new ways of looking at problems would never be found and industry would stagnate.

We know that this does not happen, so clearly we are not all slaves to the opinions of the group. Let us examine how conformity may operate so that we can be aware of the conditions which encourage creative problem-solving and innovative approaches at work.

- People are more likely to conform when they find their situation ambiguous or uncertain. When we start a new job, for example, we try to fit in – we ask others how things are done, where things are, how things work, and so on. In other words we are likely to go along with the group and try not to 'rock the boat'.

- People are more likely to conform if they value group membership. In other words, the more important the group is to us, the more likely we are to go along with the group's opinions. Psychologists call important groups *reference groups*, because we make reference to group norms and values when we form our own attitudes.

- People are more likely to conform if there is a lot of interaction among members of the group. Lieberman (1956) carried out a three-year study which showed how individuals conform to the attitudes held by their reference groups. In the first year, some factory workers were promoted to supervisor status, and others were elected to be union stewards. Eighteen months later, some of the supervisors went back to being plain factory workers because of cutbacks. Some of the stewards also returned to being ordinary workers because they chose not to run again or were defeated in the elections. Lieberman found that factory workers who were promoted to being supervisors became more pro-management and more anti-union. Those who remained as supervisors kept these attitudes, but those who returned to the factory floor changed to become anti-management and pro-union. He found the same pattern amongst the union stewards. Thus people actually change their attitudes to fit in with the group, rather than enduring the embarrassment of changing their position.

The major problem of conformity at work is that it is very difficult to go against the group as an individual. Thus you may find that you do not work as hard as you could, or you come to dislike your job because of group influence. You may be afraid to voice your opinions because you are afraid of the group's reaction. As a manager, conformity presents important problems if a good worker becomes influenced by group pressure to adopt lower standards.

What can you do? If you are in a group at work that you don't like, can you influence it? Studies of minority influence suggest that you can.

minority influence

Studies on the influence of a minority in a group show that an individual can influence the group – but to do so it is important to be seen as consistent and credible.

If the subject being considered by the group is clearly defined and easy to understand, it is less likely that the group will be influenced by a minority, but when the problem is ambiguous and complex it is more likely that the minority can influence the wider group.

When an individual consistently asserts a personal viewpoint in a confident but open way, it is likely to stimulate the rest of the group to consider that point of view. If the individual can get a supporter then his or her chances of influencing the group are greatly increased.

Just asserting a viewpoint is unlikely to be a successful strategy. The thing to do is to keep saying what you mean, but to be open to the group's view, and having done so, give clear arguments as to why you do not agree. You need to get the other group members to think about your position. Once they start to really think about what you are saying, the chances are that if your arguments are reasonable, they will come round. Groups are not totally inflexible. As Moscovici, Mugny and Van Avermaet (1985) repeatedly point out, people are *converted* by minorities, they *submit* to majorities.

over-conformity: groupthink

Janis (1972) defined groupthink as '. . . a mode of thinking that people engage in when they are deeply involved in a cohesive ingroup, when the members' striving for unanimity overrides their motivation to realistically appraise alternative courses of action'. In other words, when people are deeply committed to a group and its norms, the pressure to conform can lead them not to evaluate properly all the alternative courses of action they could take. Groupthink is a detrimental group process which needs to be avoided in organisations because once it occurs the quality of decision-making plummets. It is an example of over-conformity which tends to occur in very cohesive groups and in the face of competition or threat from another group. *Cohesiveness* means how strongly bonded together the group is as a group, or how much people feel that they belong and are involved in the group.

Tysoe (1988) lists the conditions under which groupthink is most likely to emerge:

- When the group has no traditions, or no methods, of open-mindedly searching out and evaluating information and alternative options.

- When the group is very tightly knit or cohesive.

- When the group is relatively isolated from outside information and expert opinion.

- When the group has a leader who does not promote a spirit of critical inquiry but demands group loyalty and no rocking of the boat.

- When the group is under stress.

When groupthink occurs it can be spotted by its symptoms. The most important are as follows:

1 *The illusion of invulnerability* The group feels immune to danger, and hence tends to underestimate risks and overestimate the ability to succeed.

2 *Collective rationalisation* The group members rationalise failures and try to re-define them as successes. They fail to see weaknesses in their plans. Even when they are getting feedback that things are going wrong, they tend to ignore it.

3 *Belief in the inherent morality of the group* Group members believe in the rightness of their own beliefs; they become self-righteous.

4 *Stereotypes of out-groups* Other groups, such as competing groups, are seen in a caricatured way – often they are seen as basically stupid or inept and are thus undervalued.

5 *Direct pressure on dissenters* Anyone who disagrees with the majority is pressured to conform.

6 *Self-censorship* Members of the group keep quiet about their own misgivings or doubts about the correctness of the group's actions.

7 *Illusions of unanimity* Because of self-censorship and pressure on dissenters, the group members are under the illusion that they all agree on the rightness of the group's decisions.

Groupthink is dangerous, and it is important to be aware of it. If you spot the symptoms you must at once alert the other group members to what is happening. We know from minority influence work that if you can get someone else to support you, your chances of counteracting groupthink will be increased. More usefully, you need to stop this process happening at all. First, try to keep the group discussion open – encourage people to express doubts and to share information, even when this goes against group opinions. Secondly, encourage healthy debate. Janis recommended that groups should always appoint a 'devil's advocate' to come up with counter arguments to ensure that the group fully considers all the available information.

So beware of these conditions and watch for signs of groupthink. If you see it happening, speak out.

group conflict

Conflict within the group can be destructive or constructive. It would be naive to think that conflict can be avoided.

Hunt (1981) lists some beneficial effects of conflict within a group:

1 It may introduce different solutions to the problem.

2 It can clearly define the power relationships within the group.

3 It may encourage creativity.

4 It may cause the group to focus on individual contributions rather than group decisions.

5 It can bring emotional, non-rational arguments into the open.

6 It can provide a release for long-term interpersonal conflicts and allow them to be resolved.

However, when conflict is destructive, it can

- dislocate the entire group and produce extreme positions;
- cause the group to lose sight of its objectives and focus on the immediate problem;
- lead people to adopt blocking and defensive tactics;
- result in the disintegration of the entire group;
- cause reason to become secondary to emotions.

We could say then that constructive conflict will enhance the group's performance, whereas destructive conflict needs to be avoided. To do this we need to look at communication processes within the group.

Hunt also lists behaviours that can lead to communication problems within the group:

1 *Restriction of information*   A group member implies that he or she knows the answer to a group problem, but refuses to share it.

2 *Lying*   A group member distorts the truth to preserve his or her position in the group.

3 *Paring*   The group splits into sub-groups which then fight instead of dealing with the conflict as a group.

4 *Put-downs*   Group members may 'put down' others in the group.

5 *Running away*   A group member refuses to join in – he or she

may literally leave the group, or may sulk, withdraw, or say 'I'm really not interested in this problem.'

6 *Making a noise / shouting down* One person speaks just to hold the floor – a power play to show who has control.

7 *Expertise* A group member uses expertise to stop others, such as confusing them with jargon or name-dropping: 'When I was talking to the Minister about this problem . . .'.

8 *Repressing emotions* Instead of allowing emotions to be expressed and dealt with, a group member denies the validity of the emotions, e.g. 'Let's not get emotional' or 'I suggest we all try and behave like adults.'

9 *Changing the subject* Group members avoid conflict by changing the topic under discussion.

None of these behaviours is constructive and it is a good idea to watch your own behaviour in a group to make sure that you don't do any of these things. Video recordings of groups in action can be very revealing to the participants.

On the other hand, conflict can be healthy if discussed openly and without acrimony. As we saw earlier, too much agreement is not necessarily a good thing.

There are various techniques available to help group communication such as T-groups where group members come together and openly discuss group dynamics. Such techniques are usually conducted by experienced group facilitators; that is, people who are trained to manage group dynamics – who are usually psychologists.

group polarisation

Group polarisation is another group process which occurs when people discuss issues on which they have a bias, rather than neutral topics. It is more likely to occur when discussing emotional items than factual ones, but it does still occur even then. Psychologists have found that if each group member's opinion is measured before discussion and after discussion, the group as a whole shifts towards a more extreme opinion, and not towards a more neutral opinion as might be expected.

Various explanations have been put forward as to why this effect occurs, the most likely being that group discussion makes group norms more apparent, and group members then strive to conform to the norm which is perceived as being more extreme than their own view.

When the item under discussion is a neutral one, emotionally and in terms of no-one feeling strongly one way or the other, the effect is unlikely to occur. However, when feelings run high and the issue is emotionally charged then there may well be polarisation. It is a classic example of two heads *not* being better than one, and needs to be watched for.

The way to counteract polarisation is to be aware of it and to ensure that everyone speaks out in the group. Ways to manage this are discussed in the next chapter.

===

PRACTICAL EXERCISE – Group polarisation

You need to work in a group of, say, three to five people. Before the session begins, each group member should read the passage below, and silently decide which option to endorse. Do not discuss your choice with anyone else.

Mr A, an electrical engineer who is married and has one child, has been working for a large electronics corporation since graduating from college five years ago. He is assured of a lifetime job with a modest though adequate salary and liberal pension benefits upon retirement. On the other hand, it is very unlikely that his salary will increase much more before he retires. While attending a convention, Mr A is offered a job with a small, newly founded company which has a highly uncertain future. The new job would pay more to start with and would offer the possibility of a share in the ownership if the company survived the competition of the larger firms.

Imagine that you are advising Mr A. Listed below are several probabilities or odds of the new company proving financially sound:

Each member of the group should choose the lowest probability that he or she considers acceptable to make it worth while for Mr A to take the new job. Group members should not, at this stage, discuss their choice.

- *The chances are 1 in 10 that the company will prove financially sound.*
- *The chances are 3 in 10 that the company will prove financially sound.*
- *The chances are 5 in 10 that the company will prove financially sound.*
- *The chances are 7 in 10 that the company will prove financially sound.*
- *The chances are 9 in 10 that the company will prove financially sound.*
- *Choose this option if you think that Mr A should **not** take the job, no matter what the probabilities involved.*

Now assemble as a group. Do not show the other group members your initial choice. One member of the group should read out the following instructions:

Having thought about the situation alone, we are now coming together for a group discussion of Mr A's position. We are going to discuss the problem as a group and then reach a unanimous decision about what Mr A should do. The decision **must** *be a unanimous decision and not a majority decision.*

Now discuss the problem until you all agree on one choice. Average the pre-discussion answers and compare them with your group decision. You should find that the group was more extreme than the average of individual's pre-discussion choices. If so, you have experienced group polarisation. If not, what happened? Were you alert to the possibility of polarisation?

Adapted from Kogan and Wallach, 1964

summary

▸ The mere presence of other people is enough to change our behaviour.

▸ A group consists of people who are working together to achieve some common objective.

▸ Informal groups can be a useful means of communicating in organisations.

▸ Social roles are pervasive and can affect our behaviour profoundly.

▸ Group norms form over time and are an unspoken set of rules about what is and what is not acceptable behaviour within a group.

▸ Conformity in organisations can lead to stagnation and avoidance of change.

▸ Minorities can influence the majority opinion if they are credible and persistent.

▸ Groupthink is an example of over-conformity and can lead to poor decision-making.

▸ Group conflict can be either destructive or constructive – a great deal depends on the way it is handled by the group.

▸ Group polarisation can lead to groups becoming extreme in their judgements.

suggestions for further reading

Most social psychology textbooks cover the topics in this chapter – choose a recently published one.

6. group work

We saw in chapter 5 that groups have a great deal of influence on the way that individuals work and communicate. In this chapter we explore some techniques which can help to overcome detrimental group processes such as conformity and polarisation, and which also maximise effective group decision-making. Later in the chapter we move on to look at meetings, since a lot of decision-making and problem-solving is carried out during meetings. Finally we move onto team building and development.

general principles

decision-making groups versus individuals

Popular sayings such as 'too many cooks spoil the broth' and 'two heads are better than one' show us that we are already aware of the fact that groups can be effective in some situations, whilst individuals perform better in others. How do we decide the best strategy?

participation

We know that when individuals are brought together and allowed to participate in the decision-making process, they are much more likely to accept the decision than if they are simply told what the decision is. People who participate in coming to a decision see the reasoning behind the decision, they are aware of how alternatives were considered and discarded, and they understand how the decision was arrived at. This can be important at work because all too often decisions appear to be made arbitrarily by superiors who are seen as being removed from the problems of the workplace. When this happens, employees will be slow to accept the decision and may resist its implementation.

In one interesting study, a company was trying to reduce a high rate of absenteeism. The company developed a plan for paying bonuses to counteract this, along with participating staff – it was thus a joint decision with employees playing an active role in the decision-making process. This same bonus scheme was also introduced in another part of the organisation. It was found that the scheme was not as effective when it was imposed as when it had been jointly developed with staff, even though it was exactly the same scheme. When it was imposed, staff saw it as just another management ploy; when it was agreed, staff understood the scheme better and responded far more positively.

Overall, participation can be important when the company wants to ensure that workers will be happy with a decision. But group participation is not always appropriate and should not be used without consideration of the circumstances. There are times when the individual manager is better to go it alone. Vroom and Yetton (1973) specified the conditions under which participative decision-making should be adopted:

1 When managers do not have enough information to solve the problem alone, e.g. when experts are needed, or when team members have all been working on different aspects of the problem.

2 When the nature of the problem is unclear. The group can help to define the problem and help to separate out the real problem itself and the symptoms, or effects, of the problem. For example, the manager receives several complaints that the computer department are very slow in responding to call-outs to help with computer-related problems. This in turn is causing problems in other departments that are dependent on the computer to fulfil certain tasks. By discussion with the computer manager and his staff it may be found what is actually causing the slowness in response to call-outs – perhaps the whole department has gone down with flu, or they are under-resourced. Alone, the manager could not possibly come to grips with the problem.

3 When subordinates share the manager's goals in solving the problem. (If the subordinates think that the 'best' solution is not in their own interests, then they are unlikely to go for that solution.)

4 When acceptance of the decision is necessary for its effective implementation (as discussed above).

5 When there are no pressing time constraints. Decision-making takes longer when carried out by a group than by an individual.

6 When the problem is important to subordinates.

7 When subordinates have a strong desire for independence. Some people like to be given orders and carry them out. But in environments such as Research and Development, where many workers are strong-minded and independent, participative decision-making is usually welcomed.

Participation can be beneficial to an organisation, but should not be used as a cure-all approach.

cognitive biases

When people are asked to estimate the probability or likelihood of an event occurring, or to judge the frequency with which events occur, they are influenced by the relative ease with which instances are brought to mind. The utility of this in everyday life is obvious; individuals cannot consider all instances, either because the information is not easily found, or because there are so many instances that to consider all of them would be impossible. So people use a *heuristic* to simplify the judgement task (the *availability heuristic*).

A heuristic is a strategy by which people deduce the answer on the basis of a limited number of instances. For example, if the owner of a Siamese cat was asked to estimate how many Siamese cats there are in England, it is likely that the estimate would be a far higher number than that given by the owner of, say, an Alsatian dog, because the cat owner is far more likely to know others with Siamese cats than the dog owner.

The more easily one can think of instances of a class of event, the more likely one is to judge that this is the larger class. It is not the actual number of instances that is important; it is the ease with which the instances are brought to mind. If instances are easily brought to mind, then it follows that there must be more of them. However, useful though the heuristic may be, the limited information search can lead to errors of judgement.

In decision-making groups, the group can become unduly influenced by the availability of arguments. These arguments become available in the free flow of discussion about the task at hand. It seems that the arguments which actually get discussed in groups are those which support the initial bias held by group members, whilst those that do not are discounted.

A second cognitive bias which can affect decision-making is called *epistemic freezing*. What this means is that we tend to form an opinion, and once it is formed we prefer to leave it alone; that is, we freeze our position. This is likely to happen on issues that are important to the participants. This leads to a reluctance to consider opposing arguments in any way other than a cursory acknowledgement.

It is therefore important to ensure that availability and epistemic freezing do not influence the decision-making group. Once again it is important to emphasise that *all* arguments must be considered when a group is coming to a decision.

accuracy

Generally, groups can make more accurate decisions than individuals do. Why should this be? There seem to be two main factors:

1 Bringing together a group of people also brings together a diversity of knowledge and information which is not available to one person.

2 Different people have different approaches to the problem under consideration. It is all too easy to 'get into a rut' in the way we approach problems. For example, personnel specialists look at the 'people' aspects of a problem; accountants look at the financial side of it; and so on.

However, these factors depend on diversity within the group – diversity of knowledge and diversity of approach. Simply bringing in more of the same type of person will not improve decision-making accuracy.

group composition

First, we know that *heterogeneity* is important in the group's composition. Secondly, the *knowledge* and *skills* which group members bring to the group must be relevant to the problem under consideration.

Allen and Marquis (1964) investigated engineers solving a design problem. They split the engineers into four kinds of decision-making group: the first group had only experienced success in solving similar design problems; the second group had experienced both successful and unsuccessful experiences on similar design problems; the third group had only had unsuccessful experiences; and the fourth group had no experience at all of similar design problems. They then compared how successful each group was in solving the problem. The first group correctly solved 80% of the problems set; the second group 50%; the third group 43%; and the fourth group only 25%. In this case, only the right kind of prior experience was helpful.

The third factor in group composition concerns the *status* of group members. The basic problem is that high-status group members exert a disproportionate amount of influence in the group's choice of solution to problems. Berkowitz (1986) discusses a study of three-man bomber crews who had been established for some time. They were asked to solve various problems. It was found that when the pilot (the highest-status group member) had the correct solution at the beginning, all but 6% of the crews accepted the solution. But when the lowest-status group member had the correct solution at the beginning, only about a third of the crews accepted it. Therefore the group is likely to defer to the judgement of the highest-status individual amongst them. This shows us the importance of encouraging and listening to contributions from all group members, regardless of status.

techniques for group decision-making

brainstorming

Brainstorming is a technique that is used to encourage group creativity. It was developed in 1939 by an advertising executive, Alex Osborn. Brainstorming sessions are held when companies want to generate a lot of ideas. Basically, a group of about six to ten people is assembled. It is considered unwise to include too many experts as they may have rigid ideas. Each session lasts for about an hour and begins with the chairperson making a comment such as, 'Now remember, no criticisms – we want as many ideas as possible, the wilder the better.' Osborn laid down certain guidelines for the conduct of these groups. The main ones were these:

• No criticism is allowed during the sessions.

- Wide-ranging discussion is encouraged – the wild ideas can always be toned down later.
- Quantity is encouraged – the more ideas the better.
- Combining and building upon ideas is encouraged.

During the session the group members put forward ideas which are tape-recorded and later evaluated.

The technique is still widely used today, although the evidence suggests that it actually produces fewer ideas than individuals working alone, and that groups do *not* increase creativity at all – in fact, they can inhibit it. Research suggests that *individuals* are better than groups at *generating new ideas*, but that *groups* are better than individuals at *evaluating ideas*. More recently developed techniques take account of this.

Delphi technique

In this technique the group members do not actually interact directly. There are five steps:

1 First, each group member, working alone, writes down any ideas, solutions, suggestions, etc. relevant to the problem that the group is trying to solve.

2 Each individual's output is then sent to a central location where the ideas are copied.

3 Each group member is sent a copy of the contributions of all the other group members.

4 Each group member writes down his or her reaction to the other group members' ideas, and any new ideas he or she may have. Again these are sent to the central location.

5 Steps 3 and 4 are repeated until the group agrees on a solution.

This technique takes advantage of the superiority of individuals at generating ideas and also of the superiority of groups in evaluating ideas, and is thus a very good technique, although it is time-consuming.

nominal group technique

The groups are called 'nominal' because they do not actually talk as a group for most of the process, so they are only *nominally* a group, i.e. in name only. This approach takes advantage of individual idea generation followed by a discussion of the ideas. This discussion allows information exchange which can facilitate creativity from group members 'bouncing ideas' off each other. There are five stages in the process:

1 The group members meet, but are not allowed to talk. Usually they sit around a table together. Each group member is given the problem and writes down ideas, suggestions, etc., working entirely alone.

2 Each group member in turn presents one idea to the group. This continues until all ideas have been presented.

3 The group discusses all the ideas.

4 Each group member independently ranks all the ideas, working alone.

5 The group decision is the one with the highest ranking.

As in the Delphi technique, nominal group technique uses individuals to generate ideas, and the group discusses and evaluates them. This is slightly less artificial than the Delphi technique, since group members do get a chance to discuss the ideas.

PRACTICAL EXERCISE – *Group decision-making*

The idea of this exercise is to try the three different techniques discussed above: brainstorming, the Delphi technique and nominal group technique.

Scenario
You are a team of product developers working for a large company with its headquarters in New York. The company make frozen foods. Recently they have decided to concentrate on 'healthy' foods which are low in fat, high in fibre and contain no additives or preservatives, and at the same time are not too expensive. Your job is to develop a new line of foods and suggest advertising copy which could be used to support their sale.

Split into four groups:

Group 1   *Working individually, try to generate as many ideas as you can to fulfil the requirements for the new food and advertising copy. You have 30 minutes in which to do this.*
Group 2   *Use the brainstorming technique to generate ideas for the fulfilment of the new food and advertising copy. You have 30 minutes to do this.*
Group 3   *Use the Delphi technique to generate ideas for the fulfilment of the new food and advertising copy. You have 30 minutes to do this.*
Group 4   *Use the nominal group technique to generate ideas for the*

fulfilment of the new food and advertising copy. You have 30 minutes to do this.

Groups 3 and 4 may find that 30 minutes is not long enough in which to fulfil the task. Groups may continue for longer if there is time. This will give more comparable results.

When you have all finished, compare your solutions.
- *Which is the most interesting?*
- *Did you come up with similar ideas?*
- *Discuss as a group how you felt taking part in each technique.*
- *Which is the most useful for the task?*
- *How many ideas were generated using each approach?*
- *Was there any difference in the quality of ideas generated?*

common problems in group decision-making

When a group meets to discuss a problem and is trying to reach a solution, there are a number of problems which can arise. We can divide the process into four distinct stages, each with its own set of problems.

Stage One – Problem diagnosis   Before solutions to problems can be generated, we need to specify the problem clearly. At this stage there are several common errors:

- Confusing facts with opinions.
- Confusing the symptoms of the problem with the problem itself.
- Scapegoating, i.e. trying to put the blame onto someone for the problem.
- Trying to propose solutions even before the problem is properly understood.
- Biasing the diagnosis of the problem in order to favour a preferred solution.

Stage Two – Solution generation   At this stage the group needs to discuss all possible solutions to the problem. Several kinds of error can be made:

- Suggesting solutions that have nothing to do with the problem.
- Talking about what should have been done in the past, rather than examining what can be done in the present.
- Discussing the advantages and disadvantages of a solution before all solutions have been generated.

- Going back to solutions that have been used in the past without any attempt to think of new ones.

Stage Three – Solution evaluation   At this stage all the solutions need to be examined and evaluated. Errors can arise at this stage:

- Not thoroughly thinking through the consequences of any given solution.
- Trying to bias discussion in favour of a preferred solution.
- Attacking other group members rather than focusing on the solutions themselves.
- Trying to rush along and reach a solution before all solutions are properly evaluated.

Stage Four – Solution choice   At this stage the group needs to choose one of the solutions it has been discussing. Problems can arise at this stage too:

- Confusing a silence with agreement.
- Group members trying to win an argument at the expense of a good solution.
- Steamrollering – the first solution to get attention tends to be adopted.
- High-status members choosing a solution without letting all group members voice their choices.

At all stages group members need to keep an open mind, discuss all contributions thoroughly, ensure that everyone has a chance to contribute, ignore status, and think each proposed solution through.

meetings

There are several texts available which discuss meetings, agendas, taking minutes and so on. Here we will look briefly at meetings from the social–psychological viewpoint.

Managers spend a lot of time in meetings. If the combined salaries of those around the table, plus travelling costs, were added together, it is likely that an hour's meeting could cost an organisation a fair amount of money.

One thing which can strongly influence how a meeting goes is the seating plan.

Round table (Fig. 8a)   Here all the group members are seated around a circular table. This is an excellent arrangement because it implies equality; everyone can see everyone else and thus all are able to make eye contact, and this fosters a supportive atmosphere.

Rectangular table, boss / chairperson at the top (Fig. 8b) This arrangement gives the key position to the chairperson, who is clearly in charge.

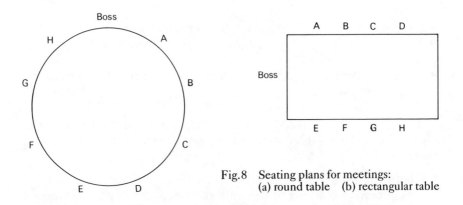

Fig.8   Seating plans for meetings:
(a) round table   (b) rectangular table

This type of arrangement encourages the group members to interact with the boss. Various effects can follow from the arrangement:

(a) *The masking effect*   The boss will find it more difficult to establish eye contact with A and E; hence they will tend to be 'masked' from getting into the conversation by the use of eye contact signals. These then are the seats for noisy and difficult participants. However, because of their proximity to the boss these seats can also be suitable for the shrinking violets who can be encouraged to contribute if the boss shifts his or her position slightly to include them by making purposeful eye contact.

(b) *The crossfire effect*   When people sit opposite each other across a table it arouses an expectation of combative interactions, so opponents should not be placed opposite each other. Instead, they will be better seated at E and H or at A and D; then they will be shielded from each other by the other participants.

(c) *The anchor-man effect*   The people at D and H are the easiest for the boss to make eye contact with. Conversely these individuals can make eye contact with several of the other participants quite easily, especially those on opposite side of the table. These seats are then useful positions for allies who can easily be cued into the conversation when the chairperson needs support.

Honey (1988) gives a useful list contrasting effective and ineffective meetings (Table 5).

Table 5   *Factors contributing to effective and ineffective meetings*

Size	Effective: about seven Ineffective: more than twelve
Frequency	Effective: maximum of once a week Ineffective: daily (familiarity breeds contempt)
Duration	Effective: maximum of 2 hours Ineffective: over 2 hours
Objectives	Effective: clear, challenging and agreed upon Ineffective: non-existent, vague
Agenda	Effective: (a) written and distributed at least 48 hours before the meeting (b) communal agenda agreed at the start of the meeting Ineffective: non-existent or not stated
Chairmanship	Effective: looks after the process, clarifies objectives and structure, summarises to check understanding Ineffective: no control, structure or summaries; lets people hog the meeting or ramble on; makes all the decisions and does all the talking
Participation	Effective: people talking in an open, honest, enthusiastic, supportive way Ineffective: some people say a lot, some say nothing
Problem-solving	Effective: systematic approach Ineffective: problems identified but not addressed; or people jumping to conclusions or solutions without an adequate discussion of the pros and cons and of the alternatives
Interruptions	Effective: none Ineffective: allowed
Conclusions	Effective: specific conclusions/actions noted so that everyone knows what to do as a consequence of the meeting Ineffective: vague or non-existent

Probably the most important person at a meeting is the chairperson. (The ins and outs of leading a group are discussed in chapter 4.) Overall, meetings are prone to detrimental group processes and many people find them a frustrating experience when they are poorly run.

team building

Teams are not quite like groups in that they are more cohesive – they can develop from groups but they do not necessarily do so.

the common task

The factor that distinguishes a team from a group is its strong cohesiveness; that is, teams are closely knit. This cohesion can lead to greater cooperation and job satisfaction. Some organisations encourage team building; the following extract describes the steel industry before automation:

'Chadwick-Jones found that crews needed a high degree of coordination to complete a cycle, and jobs were interchangeable between operatives. If men fitted into the team well they received a number of rewards in the form of additional relief breaks and increased variety through exchange of tasks. The technology determined the way the group was formed and this in turn led to a common insistence of 'harmony' and a deep feeling of team spirit amongst the men, who frequently described the works as 'home'. Every man's job in the mill was seen to be 'important'. Crews chose each other and men knew they could progress up the skill ladder with age. Crew members were firm friends, drank at the same pubs outside work and visited each other at home.' (Sidney, Brown and Argyle, 1973)

When these steelworks were automated, the teams were lost for ever. So managers can organise things to encourage a team spirit through the way the work is structured.

Here is another example from the assembly line at a light engineering factory:

'On a long assembly line morale and job satisfaction were low. One girl expressed a general feeling when she said. "It is dreadful working in such a large group; I should love to work in a small group." The nature of the work permitted one such group to exist in the department. Five other such groups were created artificially by dividing one long assembly line into five parts, with stocks in between each. Follow-up studies showed that the girls on the small line were a happy, closely-knit group. They saw the result of their work and were paid on a group-bonus scheme. The groups created by the management were the next happiest in that department, their job satisfaction was higher and they felt a greater sense of belonging, although they still felt they belonged to the larger assembly-line group. The researchers concluded that the first small group had probably derived the fullest benefits because they saw their own end product. The next best arrangement was smaller groups with intervening spaces, especially if the spatial arrangements could increase the feeling of cooperation.' (Sidney, Brown and Argyle, 1973)

Team-working on the factory floor, then, can be a successful approach for management with people working together to a common end, one that they can see and understand.

communication

Apart from working to a common end, communication between group members helps to build a cohesive team. When team members have a high degree of communication they can support each other and feel involved in what is going on. Working alone without discussion will not make people feel part of things. Proximity can be used to advantage in this situation – workers who are geographically close tend to identify with each other and bonds begin to be formed.

size

To really feel part of a group, the group should not exceed ten people. Many studies have shown that small groups out-perform larger groups and also have lower rates of absenteeism and turnover.

management and project teams

For many companies nowadays, innovative project groups, multidisciplinary research teams and project planning groups are increasingly used, particularly in technology-based industries. For such teams to work well the various roles of team members need to be considered.

Belbin (1981) identified seven roles which are useful when building management teams. When the team is to be formed from a variety of backgrounds and/or departments, one critical role is the *integrator*. The integrator pulls everyone together by solving the problems that arise as a result of these different orientations; he or she sorts out interdepartmental conflicts and smoothes the decision-making process. So the role of integrator is like that of the trouble-shooter who has no particular affiliation and whose aim is to get things running smoothly and to facilitate decision-making.

Belbin identified eight team roles:

1 *Company workers* Typically conservative, dutiful and predictable. This kind of person has a good organising ability, practical common sense, is hard working and self-disciplined.

2 *Chairperson* Typically calm, confident and controlled, the chairperson can treat everyone fairly and welcome contributions in terms of merit and without prejudice, and has a strong sense of the team's objectives.

3 *Shaper* Typically highly-strung, outgoing and dynamic, the shaper has a strong drive and is ready to challenge inertia, ineffectiveness, complacency and self-deception.

4 *Plant* Typically highly individualistic, serious-minded and unorthodox with a brilliant intellect, imagination and knowledge.

5 *Resource investigator* Typically an extrovert, enthusiastic, curious and communicative with a capacity for contacting people and exploring new areas and ideas. Also has an ability to respond to challenges.

6 *Monitor-evaluator* Typically sober, unemotional and prudent, with good judgement, discretion and a hard-headed attitude.

7 *Team-worker* Typically person-oriented, mild and sensitive with the ability to respond to people and able to promote team spirit.

8 *Completer-finisher* Typically a painstaking, orderly, conscientious and anxious person with the capacity to follow things through, and a passion for perfection.

Belbin's team types would make an ideal team. It is possible to have someone fulfilling two roles at once but this is unusual. It is suggested that one of the reasons that teams fail is that they include members who cannot be fitted into any of the roles. Some other possible reasons for team failure are as follows:

- absence of any really clever people
- personality clashes in the team
- inability of some members to fulfil their team role
- drifting back towards familiar roles and away from team roles
- inability of organisational culture to support the team.

Whilst Belbin sees team building proceeding from scratch, this is rather an 'ideal world' approach.

Dyer (1984) has suggested a team development programme for helping existing teams to work effectively together. He recommends the following:

1 The team should take at least one full day away from the workplace to work specifically on team building.

2 Each participant should consider the following questions and write down their answers for group consideration:
- What keeps you from being as effective as you would like to be in your position?
- What keeps the staff (unit or department) from functioning as an effective team?
- What do you like about this unit that you would like to maintain?
- What suggestions do you have for improving the quality of our working relationships and the functioning of our department?

3 When the group meets, each participant should read out his or her answers to the four questions above whilst another group member writes them up on a board or flipchart. This will result in four lists; the first detailing each participant's individual blocks to effectiveness, the second showing perceived blocks to team effectiveness, the third listing what is positive about the current situation in the department, and the fourth containing the suggestions for improvement.

4 The group now ranks the problems it thinks should be addressed and this list comprises the meeting agenda.

5 Now the group examines what the blocks to team effectiveness are. This may involve '. . . changing assignments, clarifying roles, clearing up misunderstandings, sharing more information, or making other innovations. The point is to engage the team in a regular examination of its own effectiveness and the development of solutions to its own problems.' (Chell, 1987)

Dyer's approach concentrates on an ongoing programme of team development. These meetings need to be held regularly so that the team is constantly reviewing its effectiveness and the blocks to effectiveness as well as individual roles within the team. Often it is appropriate to employ an outside consultant for team building since there are many approaches, of which Dyer's is only one. Others include Blake and Mouton's, and McGregor's.

summary

- Participation in decision-making can increase decision acceptability.
- Groups can increase decision accuracy if the group membership is diverse.
- Brainstorming is a group creativity technique designed to elicit several ideas.
- The Delphi and nominal group techniques are designed for creative problem-solving in groups.
- Problem-solving as a process follows four stages: problem diagnosis, solution generation, solution evaluation and solution choice. Blocks to good problem-solving can occur at any of these stages.
- The dynamics of meetings can be affected by seating arrangements.
- Teams are highly cohesive groups that can increase productivity and job satisfaction in a variety of organisational settings.
- Teams for innovation need a diverse membership. Belbin has identified certain key roles for such teams.
- Dyer has suggested a team-building technique for already existing management teams.

suggestions for further reading

Chell, E. (1987) *The Psychology of Behaviour in Organizations*, Macmillan, London. Part II concentrates on groups and teams.

Evans, D. W. (1986) *People, Communication and Organisations*, Pitman Publishing, London. Chapter 13 covers meetings: the different types, the various members' roles, agendas, and so on.

Stafford, C. (1989) *People in Business Organisations*, Cambridge University Press, Cambridge.

7. *intergroup dynamics*

Being the member of a group can strongly influence the way we behave. When groups have to communicate/negotiate/cooperate with other groups, things can become even more complicated. Groupthink (see page 77) is an example of the kind of process that occurs when a group feels threatened or has to make decisions under tight time constraints, and we should not forget it when talking about intergroup processes, because it can be triggered off by group members seeing another group as being threatening in some way. For example, members of the marketing department of company A can become subject to groupthink when planning their strategy against company B's new product. They can underestimate the potential threat from company B's product when groupthink sets in.

Funnily enough, just belonging to a group can alter the way we see our environment. The group reality acts like a kind of filter through which we look out at the rest of the world.

general principles

When one person communicates with another person there are many psychological processes which can hinder the communication process, as we have seen in previous chapters. So when a group tries to communicate with another group the problem is even more fraught with difficulties!

ingroups and outgroups

Studies have found that just allocating people to two distinct groups sets up a kind of conflict between the groups. Groups in competition develop negative views of each other as a result of intergroup discrimination. The group you belong to is called the *ingroup* and the competing group is called the *outgroup*.

In a classic study, Sherif (1962) invited 22 American boys to a summer camp. They were from similar backgrounds but did not know each other previously. The boys were randomly allocated to two different groups at the camp and lived in separate cabins. Within a week the groups were strongly established and there was a strong ingroup feeling. Each group saw the other group in a negative light and their own group as superior to the outgroup. Sherif found that the only way to overcome this intergroup hostility was to set *superordinate goals* towards which both groups had to work; that is, goals that were greater than those of the ingroup alone. For example, he made the camp truck break down some 20 miles from the camp; the only way the boys could get back was to work together and pull the truck back. By working together the intergroup hostility was overcome.

So once an ingroup and an outgroup are formed, hostile attitudes result. The only way to overcome these is to get the groups to work together towards a common end. Just communicating is not enough; in fact, communication can make things worse because the ingroup members form a *stereotype* of the outgroup members, and this guides their perception of the outgroup members.

intergroup relations within organisations

Since organisations are made up of groups, there is tremendous potential for intergroup conflict within them. Sales fights with production, personnel vies with finance, and so on. Much of this conflict results from separating people into groups of those carrying out a similar function. What the organisation actually needs is for people to cooperate in fulfilling its aims, but unless this is made clear as a superordinate goal, conflict is more likely to be the norm than cooperation.

coordinating work

One of the most common causes of conflict in organisations arises from the process of coordinating work across departments. Many tasks are processed first by one department and then by another. Consider the process of product development: first the marketing department carries out research into what consumers want; it then specifies a product for development. So production relies on marketing for input. Or consider when the company purchases some equipment for the typing pool – the purchase has to be approved by accounts, then bought by purchasing, then installed by the technicians. There is great potential for conflict here. In the first example, production may feel that marketing staff know nothing about production problems – the product specification may be expensive to manufacture. Members of production then go around muttering about how the people in marketing are trying to stick their noses into production business. Marketing in turn see producton as obstructive and old-fashioned in their thinking, and so it goes on.

This type of conflict arises as a result of *task interdependence*. That is, the output of one group becomes the input of another. The conflict arising from this will be at its worst when:

- the activities of one group are very influential for the activities of another group;
- a wide range of the activities of one group are affected by activities of another group;
- the responsibilities of each group are not clearly outlined.

PRACTICAL EXERCISE – Thinking about organisations

What you will need

- ► *A room to work in*
- ► *Pen and paper for everyone*
- ► *Two groups of people, at least three in each group*

Each group is a department in an organisation. One group represents the Accounts Department and the other represents the Computing Department. The Accounts Department has just been computerised and is encountering several problems. Computing believes that the Accounts Department is just being awkward.

*Working in groups, first list all the problems from your group's point of view (be creative!) then come together and discuss how to resolve your difficulties. Remember, the key to success is in finding a **superordinate goal** towards which each group can work. Finally, write a short report for the Personnel Manager, detailing what the problem was and how it was overcome.*

Unfortunately, some managers still think that competition is a 'good thing' and that by encouraging groups to compete they will become more productive. Of course this will not be the result of such a policy; instead, conflict increases and productivity decreases or stays the same. Research shows that when groups cooperate they usually produce more and better-quality products.

diagnosing intergroup conflict

It is not always easy to identify intergroup conflict. This is because it often shows up as two people arguing – each from a different group. Often this is put down to being a personality problem rather than an intergroup problem. Imagine that the head of Computing and the head of Accounts are constantly at each other's throats – how can we tell if it is an intergroup conflict causing their behaviour?

One strategy is to look at the past. Did these two people argue before? More importantly, did the previous heads of these departments argue? If so, it seems likely that there are some intergroup problems here and not interpersonal ones. If the two current heads argued in their previous roles, then maybe it is an interpersonal conflict. Finally, do other members of each department argue with each other? If so, then it is almost certainly an intergroup problem.

communication between organisations

An organisation is also a group, and a danger for organisations is to fall prey to such processes as groupthink and intergroup conflict. Since organisations are very often large, it is difficult to see them as a whole. Usually it is the decision-making group, such as the Board of Directors, who fall prey to such detrimental group processes. It is thus more fruitful here to restrict the discussion to smaller groups, and leave the 'macro' analysis to the sociologists.

intergroup conflict and the group

When there is intergroup conflict, there will be changes in the group dynamics of the groups involved. Listed here are some of the most common changes:

1 The group becomes increasingly concerned about the task at hand. Usually the group also becomes more formal – group needs come first and individuals are secondary. So everyone works like mad to do whatever it is and there is pressure for the group to perform well.

2 Loyalty to the group also becomes important. Talking to members of the outgroup is seen as treacherous, and norms are enforced more strongly. An 'all for one and one for all' attitude is common.

3 Group leaders become more autocratic and less democratic. This is because there is no time to discuss things and also because the group tends to accept strong leadership in the face of a threat.

4 The group becomes more cohesive and past differences are forgotten – there is an air of 'we must all stick together'.

5 The group distorts perception – the outgroup is denigrated and the ingroup is bolstered. That is to say, the outgroup may be seen as inferior to the ingroup (e.g. '. . . they [the outgroup] don't know the meaning of work . . .').

6 There is a shift to a win–lose orientation. So people concentrate on 'us' versus 'them', rather than 'us' versus 'the problem'. Also, everything is evaluated in terms of winning or losing *vis-à-vis* the other group, which leads to an emphasis on the benefits of winning and a tendency to ignore the consequences of the conflict in the long term.

7 Hostility to the outgroup increases and communication decreases. Even when there is communication it tends to be unsatisfactory and guided by group members' stereotypes.

Clearly then it is important to try to organise things so that such severe conflicts do not arise. Groups need to be encouraged to work in a cooperative manner, not a competitive one. One way that managers can achieve this is by rewarding cooperation between groups and emphasising organisational goals, i.e. superordinate goals.

negotiating and bargaining

If a negotiation is needed, then we can be almost certain that there is some sort of conflict between the parties involved, i.e. intergroup conflict. In this section we examine the skills needed to be an effective negotiator, although these skills are not only useful for negotiating. Refer also to chapters 2 and 5, on non-verbal behaviour and interpersonal skills – after all, in a negotiation we deal with other people.

Morley (1981) suggests that negotiating is a process with certain essential characteristics; it is not the same as arguing because it is a form of joint decision-making; conflict is an essential ingredient; negotiators try to achieve private goals; and each party may misrepresent its position in an attempt to outwit the opponents. Put simply, negotiation is designed to get others to do what you want them to do.

A successful negotiator is someone who not only achieves his or her own objectives but also negotiates an agreement that will *last* and be adhered to by both sides.

Studies have shown that when the participants are good communicators the negotiation tends to be more mutually profitable.

Negotiations seem to go through stages (Table 6). First, the two sides emphasise their points of disagreement and conflict – these need to be thoroughly explored and understood by both sides. In the second stage the interaction becomes more spontaneous as representatives look for points on which they can agree, and freer discussion takes place. Finally comes the stage when offers are made and considered by each side.

Table 6   *The three negotiating stages*

Stage of negotiation	Characteristics	Skills needed
Stage 1	Where do we stand?	Assertion; active listening
Stage 2	Wide discussion	Assertion; active listening; bridging; persuading
Stage 3	Offers/compromises	Assertion; active listening; bridging; persuading; moving away

Scott (1986) identifies five stages in negotiations:

1 *Exploration*   This is like stage 1 in Table 6, when each party states what areas it believes should be covered, what it wants and what it sees as the priorities. The response to these statements should be to ask questions to clarify the situation, but not to force the other party into a justification of its position; this sets the party up to be defensive and competitive.

2 *Joint assessment*   '. . . a co-operative and creative stage in which the parties look to see what together they can do in their joint interests'. Here the two parties need to be open and able to place their self-interest within the context of joint interest.

3 *Bidding* When bidding we need to ask several questions:
- How much shall I bid?
- How shall I make the bid?
- How should I respond to an offer?

When considering how much to bid, go for the highest defensible position, since once voiced it cannot be taken back; also, this bid creates expectations on the part of the other side as to where they can expect the negotiation to finish. For the bidder, then, the higher the bid the better – within reason! It is bound to be tested by the other party, so it must be justifiable. How do I put it?

Always state a bid clearly, firmly and without justification. When responding, again it is better to go for asking for clarification if needed, but not to respond with a counterbid; give yourself thinking time. In the meantime you may work on reducing the opposition's bid and on gaining concessions.

4 *Bargaining* If you need to make concessions, ensure that you too get some concessions from the other party. Use breaks/recesses for thinking time. Do not be pushed into letting the pace get too fast; keep it cool and measured.

5 *Settlement* Scott discusses two ways of dealing with this stage:
(a) The final push, i.e. one final concession which seals the deal. This must not be done too soon or settlement will not be reached; nor must it be done too late or the deal may be lost.
(b) 'The last ha'penny' – even when the other party offers a final concession, some negotiators are not happy until they have demanded one final small concession; otherwise they feel that they might have settled too easily. In other words, it always pays to have a little something up your sleeve to clinch the agreement.

Let us now turn to the skills that are needed for a negotiating situation.

negotiating skills

These can be broken down into five main types of skill – persuading, asserting, bridging, finding common ground, and moving away. We will look at each of these in turn.

Persuading

Since both sides will have different views, it seems pretty obvious that the representatives will try to persuade the other side of the validity of their own viewpoint. Persuading means two main things – *proposing* and *reasoning*.

Proposing is a rather neutral approach which emphasises *rationality* – it means putting forward ideas and suggestions, along the lines of 'I suggest we look at the points we can agree on first and then consider those on which we do not agree.'

Reasoning means putting forward reasons and arguments, facts and figures which support one's own view or oppose the view of the other side. For example, 'These figures show that our plans can fulfil your budget requirements and meet our time scales.' It is a very important behaviour in negotiating. This is how we build up a case and whittle away the opponent's position.

It is important to remember that persuading alone is unlikely to lead to an agreement because negotiation usually means compromise between the two parties, rather than one side persuading the other side.

When making proposals it is more effective to keep them *simple* and *direct*. When reasoning, use only a few strong arguments – skilled negotiators hold back one or two very strong arguments in reserve. Unskilled negotiators seem to think that throwing lots of average arguments at the opposition will be sufficient. It isn't! All that happens is that the opposition demolishes your average arguments, leaving you without a leg to stand on.

We also know that less skilled negotiators tend to exaggerate. Honey (1988) points out that they say things like 'very generous offer' or 'an offer you simply can't refuse' when discussing their own proposals, whereas when describing the proposals of the opposition they use terms like 'a derisory offer' or 'laughable'. This kind of approach merely serves to irritate the other side and is *not* recommended!

Asserting

This is a rather tough approach, but it is essential in bargaining and negotiating. The first behaviour is stating your expectations, saying what *you* want out of the negotiation. It is important to state what you want (or more) since the bolder you are, the more you are likely to get, so long as you are not being unreasonable. Do not confuse 'asserting' with 'assertiveness', which is a much nicer approach!

The second behaviour is evaluating the opposition – this needs to be done with caution and only really when you want to put up a show of strength. It means judging the other side explicitly and implying that you are superior. For example, 'That is a completely ridiculous demand' or 'I'm afraid we can't give in to such unreasonable demands' or 'At last you've decided to come round to a more reasonable view.' Save this for when you need to sharpen up the conflict; otherwise avoid it.

The third behaviour under asserting concerns pressuring the opposition and offering deals. Pressuring means statements like 'It's up to you – take it or leave it', or 'That's our last offer'. Offering deals would include statements like 'If you can go along with us on this point then I think we've got a deal', or 'Why don't you go along with us on this and we could reconsider clause two?' Again, this can be a risky move, but it is at the heart of bargaining and negotiating. The important thing is only to offer concessions after the other side has, not before, or it can be seen as a sign of weakness.

Bridging

This is all about forming bridges beween you and the opposition. Firstly it includes *involving* and *supporting* behaviours. These are extremely important in negotiating and are used extensively by skilled negotiators. Basically, you ask questions in order to find out what the other's goals and positions are: for example, 'Can you tell me what problems you have with this?' You show support for the other side's fairness and reasonableness, thus harnessing the powers of self-fulfilling prophecy on your side; for example, 'I'm sure you wouldn't say that without good reason', or 'That seems a very fair evaluation of the situation'. By using these tactics, the negotiator is buying time, pacing the interaction and finding out how the other side is thinking. This gives you time to plan. Skilled negotiators ask at least twice as many questions as average ones.

The second set of behaviours in bridging is *disclosing*. This means making your own motives and reactions clear to the other side, and needs to be used carefully to build trust. Clearly, you do not disclose just anything! However, disclosing is useful because the other side feels more secure and this can help to build a situation in which agreement can be reached. For example, Rackham and Carlisle (1978) give this illustration of disclosing feelings:

'I'm uncertain how to react to what you've just said. If the information you've given me is true then I would like to accept it, yet I feel some doubts inside me about its accuracy. So part of me feels happy and part feels rather suspicious. Can you help me resolve this?'

Here, the speaker is using disclosing to slow things down too; the other side has made the proposal. Instead of coming straight back with a counter-proposal, the speaker is trying to reduce ambiguity, slow down the pace and gain information as well as revealing something of his feelings.

The third set of behaviours included under bridging are *active listening skills*. Again these are extremely important. These include re-phrasing and repeating back what the other side has said in order to check that you have clearly understood; summarising points of agreement; and communicating acceptance of other people's feelings. The effective negotiator tests understanding and summarises far more than the average negotiator.

Taken together, bridging skills are the key to successful negotiation, and they should be studied well. By using them you establish a line of communication with the other party, you ascertain what they are thinking, and you can gain time to think by judicious use of paraphrasing and summarising.

Finding common ground

This is tremendously important – skilled negotiators spend more time looking for areas of agreement than average negotiators do. Once the habit of agreement is developed in a negotiation then more agreement is likely to follow.

When disagreements do occur, the skilled negotiator will give reasons for disagreeing first and then actually say, '. . . and so I disagree'. Thus the *reasons* are the focus of attention for the listener, and not the idea of disagreement.

Since the positions taken by the two sides are almost invariably incompatible, the skilled negotiator learns to focus on what lies behind the position. Honey (1988) calls this focusing on *interests* and not *positions* – the interests are the reasons for the other side taking up their position. He gives the example of a position of 'I must have a promotion within six months' – the interests behind such a position might be that the person wants to have a more challenging job; to have extra responsibility; to earn more money; and to qualify for a company car. Very often these interests can be met if they are known.

So we can say that positions can mask the real requirements of the negotiators.

Moving away

There are two aspects to moving away – *avoidance* and *disengagement*. Avoidance is not an effective behaviour in negotiating – it can mean backing down under pressure or changing your position when you see conflict looming; in other words, it is a defensive tactic to avoid disagreeable confrontation with the other side.

Disengagement, on the other hand, is a useful tactic; examples might be calling a break for coffee or to discuss plans with team members, or using humour to lighten the atmosphere, or changing the subject. All in all it can prevent the negotiator from becoming too tired or pressured. It can also be useful if the discussions are getting nowhere or are not constructive because everyone is tired or if things are getting petty. It can help to pace the negotiation and conserve energy.

GROUP DISCUSSION

1 What do skilled negotiators do?

2 Discuss the stages of a negotiation and the interpersonal skills needed at each stage.

3 Design a training programme for personnel who wish to become negotiators. Include non-verbal behaviour, interpersonal skills and specific negotiating skills. Summarise your ideas in a series of recommendations for the Board of Directors.

---

summary

- Simply belonging to a group can lead to intergroup discrimination.
- Much conflict in organisations arises as a result of task interdependence.
- When there is intergroup conflict, certain changes take place in the group which can be detrimental to good work performance.
- Cooperative orientations rather than competitive ones should be encouraged in organisations.
- Negotiations take place in a context of intergroup conflict.
- Each side will be prey to processes resulting from intergroup conflict, such as groupthink.
- A negotiation usually goes through three stages; at each stage different skills are appropriate.

▸ There are five main categories of negotiating skills: persuading, asserting, bridging, finding common ground, moving away.
▸ Skilled negotiators learn to pace the negotiation by asking questions, taking breaks when needed, and listening hard to the opposition.
▸ Skilled negotiators are tough. When necessary they will use asserting skills.
▸ Skilled negotiators summarise often and check back their understanding of the other side's position.
▸ Skilled negotiators look for common ground, not for disagreements.
▸ Skilled negotiators are not afraid to move away from situations to allow time for feelings to cool and to re-consider their own and the other party's positions.

suggestions for further reading

Atkinson, G. M. (1975) *The Effective Negotiator*, Quest, London. A very interesting book with numerous suggestions on how to negotiate in the 'real world'.

Feldman, D. C. and **Arnold, H. J.** (1983) *Managing Individual and Group Behaviour in Organizations*, McGraw-Hill Inc., Tokyo. See chapter 19 for discussion of intergroup conflict.

8. *interviewing skills*

Interviewing is a special sort of face-to-face interaction in which the interviewer is trying to get information from the person being interviewed (the interviewee). The interviewee may also be trying to get information from the interviewer in some circumstances; for example, at a job interview the interviewee will want to know about the job and about the conditions of work, the organisation, and so on.

All kinds of interview are conducted at work: selection interviews, job evaluation interviews, disciplinary interviews, interviews to find out what people think about an organisation's products/services/company image, leaving interviews, and so on. But with all interviews there are certain skills which are helpful. Once again it is worth looking back to chapter 1 – many of the topics discussed there are relevant to the interview.

PRACTICAL EXERCISE

Refer back to chapter 1 and identify how each of the topics is or is not relevant to the interviewing situation.

general principles

interviewing style

Managers spend a great deal of their time in face-to-face interactions with other people, and interviewing is a key skill. Some interviews are more formal than others.

Biddle and Evenden (1980) suggest that there are three styles that the interviewer can adopt: directive, patterned and non-directive.

The *directive* style means that the interviewer asks questions, keeps control, keeps to a plan and talks quite a lot. The *patterned* style is used when interviewing an equal; it has a flexible plan, with both participants doing about the same amount of talking, and would be used for appraisal interviews or maybe promotion interviews. The *non-directive* style is time-consuming, has no plan, and the interviewee does most of the talking. It is used to explore issues – maybe sensitive problems – and is used mostly for counselling purposes. In a work context the most common are the directive and the patterned styles of interviewing.

asking questions

There are also different ways of asking questions. Biddle and Evenden identify six types:

1 *Closed questions*   These are questions which close off the possibilities for the interviewee to answer so that usually he can only reply 'yes' or 'no'.
Example: 'Can you type?', 'Do you enjoy taking on responsibility?'

2 *Leading questions*   These lead the interviewee to reply in a way that pleases the interviewer and rarely yields any useful information.
Example: 'In this organisation we prefer people who like taking on responsibility. You do enjoy responsibility, don't you?'

3 *Controlling questions*   These are used by the interviewer to keep the interviewee on the topic, and stop him or her from discussing issues which are not relevant to the task at hand.
Example: 'Thank you for telling me about your hobbies. Could you tell me about your work experience?'

4 *Probing or building questions*   These ask for more information about a topic already under discussion, or build upon information already given.
Example: 'What is it you particularly like about jobs which involve responsibility?' or 'What did you mean when you said you liked to take on responsibility?'

5 *Open-ended questions*   These are the opposite to closed questions. They do not constrain the interviewee – in fact they encourage a longish response.
Example: 'Tell me about your hobbies.'

6 *Reflecting questions*   These reflect back what the interviewee has already said and are used to test understanding.
Example: 'So you play squash every week, do you?'

Directive interviews will contain more closed and leading questions, whilst a patterned style will have leading, controlling, probing and open-ended questions. A non-directive interview will mainly comprise open-ended and reflecting questions.

spit, smile or swallow?

A good interviewer tries to produce a 'smile' response from the interviewee – that is, a positive response.

'Spit' means producing anger in the interviewee by being unfriendly, unfair, rude, and so on. 'Swallow' means making the interviewee worried or tense and is produced by rudeness, disagreement or threat.

An interviewer should try to create a good atmosphere, one in which the emotional content is positive and constructive.

conducting the interview

preparation

- Before you conduct an interview it is essential to be *prepared* for it. This often involves reading relevant material, e.g. application forms, personnel reports, etc. Ask yourself what facts you need to know before starting.
- You also need to think about *why* you are conducting the interview; that is, what is your *objective*? Say to yourself, 'What result do I want to achieve by the end of this interview?' Without an objective you will not be able to say whether or not the interview was successful.
- You may want to prepare an *interview plan* beforehand. This may be as simple as a few notes about particular areas you want to explore, or as detailed as allocating, say, five minutes for discussion of previous work experience, five minutes for questions from the candidate, and so on. Keep your objective in mind when planning.
- Choose *where* and *when* you are going to conduct the interview. Will it be in your office, in the reception area, in the personnel department? Should it be first thing in the morning to get it over

with, or last thing so that you can let it run as long as is necessary? The room in which you interview can affect the way things go – a very formal set-up with a desk between you and the interviewee may inhibit younger people and intimidate them. Conversely, low chairs and tables, with coffee and biscuits, can encourage people to talk more freely.

- Brief other people not to interrupt you during the interview. You may need to have your phone switched through to someone else.

the welcome stage

The interviewee has arrived for the interview. The first few minutes are vital to setting the stage for the rest of the interaction. What you are aiming for here is to put the interviewee at ease so that he or she is prepared to talk openly and truthfully.

Usually this stage begins with some informal chat such as asking if the interviewee has had a good journey, is well, and so on. You should then explain the way you see the interview going, by clarifying the procedure you intend to follow. This establishes the ground rules. For example: 'I would like to spend a few minutes going over your past employment history before we go on to discuss how you might fit in here. Then perhaps you might like to ask me some questions about our set-up. Is there anything you would like to know before we begin?'

The timing of this stage will vary with individual circumstances. If you already know the interviewee, it could make him or her uneasy if the interview does not get to the point quickly. On the other hand, if your interviewee is young and nervous it may help to get him or her talking if you first discuss one of their hobbies, or school perhaps, before getting down to business.

acquiring information

The main skill here is to keep the conversation on course so that you can find out what you need to know. In other words, you must be in control of what is happening. To do this you ask questions.

Open-ended questions encourage the interviewee to talk freely. Closed questions re-establish the interviewer's control. A typical exchange might go something like this:

Q. What was it that attracted you to this job?

A. It was mainly that I felt it would give me the opportunity to use my management skills and to take on increased responsibility.

Q. What sort of things do you have in mind?

A. Well, at the moment my boss is rather controlling and I always have to refer everything to him. I prefer more freedom to make my own decisions.

We can see here that the interviewee wants more autonomy in a job and feels ready for promotion. The interviewer builds on the first answer to ask the next question, thus giving an easy flow to the interaction. Generally it is a good idea to start with an open-ended question and then to follow up from there.

Reflective questions can be useful at this stage, for example, 'You enjoyed that part of your job?' Keep these gentle, or they can sound accusing. Ask the question in a friendly and supportive way, to encourage the interviewee to be open and to protect him or her from fear of losing face.

Make sure that you listen carefully – after all, it is only common courtesy to do so – and listen too to the tone of voice, the pauses, the emotional nuances. Hesitation can mean uncertainty, sudden emotion could be a signal that you need to know more about the subject. It is important not to spend all the time thinking about what to ask next, but to try to let it flow from the conversation. If you have done your preparation you should have no difficulty here.

Watch the interviewee's body language. Is he or she tense? Defensive? Watch your own too – lean slightly forward, look at the interviewee, show interest and concern for what he or she is saying. There's nothing worse than being interviewed by someone who is always looking at notes or out of the window!

supplying information

At some point in the interview, the interviewee can expect *you* to supply information. Be open, and answer any questions with courtesy and as much information as it is possible to give.

parting

Eventually the interview is over and nothing more of use can be gleaned. It is the interviewer's job to conclude the session.

You should summarise any agreements made to ensure that you both agree on what has transpired. The interviewee should leave feeling that he or she has had a fair hearing.

after the interview

- Make any notes right away. Do not delay – it is surprising how quickly you can forget exactly what happened.
- Does anyone else need to be informed about the outcome of the interview? If so, make sure you get in touch with them via the appropriate channels.
- If there is any action you need to take, such as sending a letter to the interviewee or taking up references, do it now.
- Finally, spend five minutes going over what happened in your mind. Could you have handled things any better? Did you achieve your objective? If not, why not?

the selection interview

No discussion of interviewing would be complete without some discussion of the selection interview. It is almost unknown for a company to employ someone without an interview.

Interview procedures vary widely. Sometimes a panel of interviewers is used; sometimes there is a series of interviews lasting all day; some companies combine psychological testing with interviews.

We know that the behaviour of the interviewer will have a significant impact on how the interviewee behaves. It is important that the interviewer tries to maintain a consistent approach across all the interviews for any one job, so that the information and responses can be compared fairly.

The main task of the selection interview is to try to find out if the candidate is suitable for the job under discussion and whether he or she will fit in with the organisational culture. The candidate will also learn about the organisation and may have to be persuaded to take the job.

Interviewing as a technique for job selection has been criticised. After all, the interviewer has plenty of information already from the application form or c.v., but nothing can really replace the information that a skilled interviewer can obtain about the candidate's interpersonal behaviour and ability to fit in with the organisation, and the motivation to work.

Selection interviews can last for anything from ten minutes to over an hour. Generally, panel interviews are very stressful for the candidate and should be replaced with a sequence of individual interviews if possible. It is usually considered to be good practice for the applicant to be interviewed by at least two people separately, for comparison and to avoid bias, as well as to give two samples of behaviour.

preparation

Before seeing the candidate the interviewer should first of all study the job specification, from which a general description of the type of person needed can be built up. The interviewer should then study the application form and/or c.v. and any other available information.

As an interviewer you should also consider if you want to administer any psychometric tests, and discuss this with your personnel department, who can advise on what is available and/or suitable. Many tests need to be administered by trained personnel, so it is worth thinking about this aspect well in advance of the interview.

the interview

We know that first impressions count. Does the candidate? Did he or she take the care to dress appropriately for the interview? If not, what does that tell us about the candidate's motivation to do the job?

Tiffin and McCormick (1970) give a useful list of techniques to bear in mind when interviewing:

- The interviewer usually does not ask questions that can be answered by 'yes' and 'no'. Rather, the questions are worded so that the candidate has to talk. (See page 112, 'Asking questions'.)
- The interviewer pauses for at least a few seconds after the candidate appears to have finished, and before the interviewer asks more questions, in order to give the candidate a chance to talk further.
- The interviewer should try several different subjects at the beginning to determine which subject is most provocative in

getting the applicant to talk, but returns to those topics on which the applicant froze in order to see if the lack of response is significant in any way.

- The interviewer repeats part of the key sentences of the applicant in a questioning tone, indicating a need for elaboration.
- The interviewer asks one question at a time.
- Questions should be clear, without any indication of what the correct answer may be (if any).
- The interviewer's manner is interested, attention uninterrupted, and neither manner nor words imply criticism or impatience, or a critical attitude towards what is being said.
- The interviewer should not ask highly personal questions until a rapport has been established.
- The interviewer does not bring the candidate abruptly back to the point when the candidate digresses.
- The interviewer should use language which is appropriate for the candidate.

The candidate's record needs to be carefully explored. The information to be discussed can be classified into four main categories:

Work history

1 Discuss the candidate's duties in previous jobs. This will give some indication of how likely he or she is to be able to handle the current duties of the vacancy. Likes and dislikes will also be relevant – he or she may hate answering the telephone, which is not too helpful if the vacancy involves many telephone calls. Past achievements will be interesting and give an indication of how motivated the candidate is to succeed at work – is he or she ambitious? Past level of salary should be looked into – and beware: many candidates tend to exaggerate previous earnings levels – this can be cross-checked when references are taken up.

2 Why has the candidate changed jobs in the past? It is possible to find out some interesting things from this. For example, listen for mentions of personality clashes – once or twice is perhaps acceptable, but if it has happened too often, then it seems likely that there is something about this candidate that can mean he or she finds it difficult to work with others. This may not mean that the organisation would not want to employ that person, but it may mean that he or she needs to work alone for the most part.

3 Has the candidate changed jobs frequently? If so, it is likely that he or she won't stay long in the new job either unless

something significant is being offered which was lacking in previous jobs.

4 Are there gaps without employment? What happened? Perhaps the candidate is resourceful and trekked across Africa with only a rucksack for company, in which case so long as the travelling bug is out of his or her system, this candidate should make an interesting employee. Gaps can be worrying though, and should be checked out.

5 Finally, what would the candidate's ideal job be? Try to match this to the demands of the vacancy. You cannot, of course, expect a perfect fit, but if the candidate wants autonomy and the job is closely supervised, for example, then you might think again about his or her suitability.

From the work history you can get a good idea of certain basic characteristics: How motivated is the candidate? Does he or she have initiative?

Education and training

It can be useful to find out what the candidate's best and worst subjects were, the kinds of grades achieved, and to discuss extra-curricular activities. From this sort of information you can tell something about the abilities of the person. The extra-curricular involvement can be very useful. Does he or she go mountain climbing/walking/play squash/golf/chess? This sort of thing tells you about what the person really likes doing. Perhaps the candidate organises some kind of club – this may mean that an organisational ability has gone unnoticed and could be used. In other words, this information can tell you something of the candidate's initiative and motivation levels and level of self-discipline.

Home background

It is as well to tread carefully on this topic, but it can be useful to find out how stable the candidate is and whether, for example, he or she may not want to be away because there are young children or, perhaps, an invalid spouse at home.

Current social adjustment

This includes current interests and hobbies, health, financial status. The interviewer is really looking here for stability, good health (worth checking) and whether the candidate is financially stable – money worries can cause many problems and decrease motivational levels if unresolved.

Personality

Here you are looking for a match between the interviewee's personality and the requirements of the job. The sort of things you may want to look for are maturity, emotional stability, whether the candidate is a teamworker or an individualist, self-discipline, conscientiousness, initiative, self-confidence, honesty and sincerity.

after the interview

Leave yourself a few minutes to think back over what happened and to make notes. It is always a good idea to take up references to cross-check the validity of the information acquired during the interview. After all, if the candidate is dishonest at interview, can he or she be trusted in the job? Nowadays it is usually acceptable to telephone the referee first just to check information. Also, the more informal approach can often be far more productive than sending out standard reference forms. People are often more willing to chat about a candidate than they are to commit anything to paper. But remember – the referees were chosen by the candidate. They should be the candidate's bosses from two previous jobs if at all possible; if the candidate names other people, ask yourself/the candidate why. Ask about absenteeism – it is unlikely that the candidate will admit to often being absent from work himself.

other types of interview

These may be used in special situations and are not in routine use.

the stress interview

This is seldom used in industry. It was most used during the war by the Office of Strategic Services in the selection of people for intelligence and similar activities. You would use it now if the candidate is likely to be exposed to stress during the job. There are various techniques; for example, the interviewer may suddenly change from being friendly and relaxed to being aggressive and hostile. The candidate's reaction is watched and noted, after which the interviewer resumes a friendly manner, allowing the candidate to regain confidence and allowing the interviewer to see how well the candidate recovers from the experience. Another technique is the hard/soft approach where two interviewers take on opposite roles, one friendly and the other hostile. Having two interviewers allows observation and is designed to throw the candidate off balance.

the group interview

This brings several candidates together. Sometimes the participants are set a problem to solve together, as in the popular 'survival' scenarios, the aim being to see who leads and how well the candidates work together. (Are they good teamworkers?) Or candidates are asked to discuss a topic whilst observers rate their behaviour. This technique can be useful where leadership qualities are important or the ability to work as a team is required.

being interviewed

Let us look now at how *you* can do well at an interview. You know now how the interviewer will see things. How can *you* be successful?

preparation

Before you go to the interview you need to be prepared. The company should send you a job description and some details about the company. What you need to do now is to find out what the company does or makes, in what direction it is going. If you have been recruited by an employment agency you should find that they can give you background information; otherwise you may find that the company's public relations officer can help, or the personnel department. Do not be afraid to ask – it shows that you are interested and motivated.

Consider what you are going to wear – a suit is always fairly safe. Make sure that you are well presented. Show that you have made an effort.

Do not look on the interview as something to dread – *relax*, this is your chance to shine. Think about your career history and prepare for some of the standard questions:

- Why are you leaving your present job?
- Where do you see your career going?
- What do you like doing?
- Why should the company want *you*?
- What *benefits* can you offer them?
- How can you help them?

121

the interview

If you are well dressed you should feel relaxed – you look the part. *Never* arrive late – give yourself plenty of time to get there (you can always have a cup of coffee somewhere). Answer all questions fully and truthfully. Try to enjoy the interview – it's your chance to show what you can do. Always remember: they want to recruit someone, you want the job. All you have to do is convince them that *you can do it* and *you want to do it*. If you feel either that you cannot do the job or don't want the job, you shouldn't be there. Good luck!

PRACTICAL EXERCISE – *Mock interviews*

What you will need
▶ *Three people to take part: one to be the interviewer, one to be the interviewee and one to be an observer*
▶ *Pen and paper*

What to do
You are going to conduct a mock interview. It could be a selection interview, a job evaluation interview, a careers counselling interview. You choose a topic that interests you.

Before you conduct the mock interview, allow ten minutes for the interviewer and interviewee to prepare.

The observer does not take part. He or she records what is going on, using the table below.

Observer checklist
Put a tick in the frequency box each time you hear the type of question.

Type of question	Frequency
Closed questions	
Leading questions	
Controlling questions	
Probing / building questions	
Open-ended questions	
Reflecting questions	

At the end of the interview, count up how many times the interviewer used each type of question. Refer back to this text to see whether the interview was **directive, patterned** *or* **non-directive.**

As a group, discuss how the interview went.
- *Did the interviewer use the appropriate style?*
- *Was the interviewee at ease?*
- *Was the interviewer well prepared?*
- *Did he or she allow the interviewee to answer fully?*
- *Did he or she listen carefully?*

GROUP DISCUSSION

1 *Discuss how you would go about training someone to be an interviewer.*
2 *What is the importance of non-verbal behaviour in interviews?*

summary

▸ It has been suggested that there are three styles which the interviewer can adopt: directive, patterned, non-directive.
▸ There are at least six ways of asking questions: closed, leading, controlling, probing, open-ended, reflecting.
▸ Before holding an interview, it is essential to prepare properly.
▸ Interviews can be said to have discrete stages: preparation, welcome, acquiring information, supplying information, parting, reflection on what happened.
▸ Selection interviewing is one of the commonest forms of interviewing carried out at work and is a skilled procedure.
▸ Four main types of information need to be covered in a selection interview: work history, education and training, home background, current social adjustment.

suggestions for further reading

Sidney, E. and **Brown, M.** (1973) *The Skills of Interviewing*, Tavistock, London. A practical book for personnel and management.

Ungerson, B. (ed.) (1975) *Recruitment Handbook*, second edition, Gower Press, Aldershot. Covers job interviewing – how to prepare job specifications, advertising, references. Good source book for selection.

9. *technological communication*

This chapter concerns communicating via technological means. The telephone has long been a part of business life and is essential to effective business communication. However, computers now offer many opportunities for communication, as do the sophisticated teleconferencing facilities offered by modern telecommunications equipment.

Since technological developments are currently so rapid, the aim of this chapter is not to detail each kind of communication system – it would be out of date before the book went to press! Instead, we concentrate on the psychological issues involved with this type of communication.

Strangely enough, some kinds of system – for example, videoconferencing – have not taken off, although they seem appealing. We shall look briefly at why this is so and how each type of system is most useful. The way that you choose to communicate (by phone/by networked computer system, etc.) can be important and can affect what you are trying to achieve (the task).

general principles

We can distinguish between *mediated* and *non-mediated communication*, where mediated communication refers to any communication between one or more people that involves a medium through which the communication is channelled (e.g. a letter, a phone call). Non-mediated communication means face-to-face meetings where people can talk directly to each other.

Mediated communication introduces a new dimension into the communication process and it is the effect of so doing that is the concern of this chapter.

social presence

Short, Williams and Christie (1976) first put forward the concept of social presence. Basically, if we are talking face to face we could say that this represents the highest level of social presence, whilst communicating by letter represents a very low level of social presence.

Social presence is about a feeling of how 'close' the other person is physically. It is a reflection of the feeling of closeness of the other. In face-to-face meetings the social presence of the other person is high and so we treat that person as real flesh and blood. All non-verbal communication is present, as are the social pressures towards avoiding conflict and avoiding too high a level of emotion. We all know that it can be easier to communicate by letter or telephone, especially if there is a conflict. It is easier to lay out our position when we don't actually have to face the other person.

In a similar way, mediated communication with lower social presence can make it easier to state a position or take a formal, impersonal view and to avoid compromising. This can make these media good substitutes for some types of interaction.

When the interaction calls for good interpersonal skills like assessing another person, persuading or negotiating and bargaining, mediated communication may not be the best option. The outcome could be different depending on whether the meeting is face to face or mediated.

communicating by telephone

When we talk with someone over the telephone, the most important difference from a face-to-face discussion is that we cannot see the other person. Hence we lose many of the non-verbal behaviours that support conversation. So, for example, we cannot tell if the other person is smiling or frowning. It can be difficult to establish a 'rapport'. with the other person because of the loss of the non-verbal signals which normally support interactions. Let us look at some of the advantages and disadvantages of using the telephone.

At work it is perfectly possible to know someone only through telephone conversations and never actually to meet them. We have probably all experienced surprise sometimes when we have met someone with whom we have only communicated over the phone – our mental picture turns out to be completely different from the reality of seeing the person in the flesh. The point to watch here is that we may form impressions of the other person which are not accurate, so we must not rely on them.

In the absence then of many of the cues we usually use to assess someone face to face, we pay far more attention to what is said and how it is said when talking on the telephone. However, because of the absence of visual cues, we are also more likely to be distracted when on the phone; we see someone come into the office and allow our thoughts to wander – why have they come in, what are they doing, and so on; suddenly we realise we haven't heard a word of what the caller is saying.

Apart from the possibility of being distracted, our conversational partner may also be distracted by events around him or her, so we must not assume that we have their undivided attention, nor that it is a convenient time to call. The initiator of the telephone call should always ask first if it is a convenient time to talk.

Since there is no visual aspect to a telephone conversation, it is more difficult to remember information communicated in this way – this plus the distraction problem means that it is a good idea to take notes of telephone conversations either during the call or immediately afterwards.

Communication is also hampered by the reliance on the spoken word. All information must be imparted this way without documentary support, so if reference is being made to documents, they should always be at hand for both parties.

Finally, research shows that it is more difficult to detect deception over the phone than it is face to face – although this finding is slightly dubious. However, it is worth bearing in mind. If there is any suspicion that the other person is likely to try to deceive, it is as well to insist on a face-to-face meeting. This way, you can see the other person's non-verbal behaviour, which may help you to tell if he or she is being truthful. (Note that avoiding eye contact and using the hand to cover the mouth are both possible indicators of deception.)

On the other hand, the telephone provides an easy way of

communicating with others, both near and distant. We are used to the telephone and doing business without it seems almost impossible (Table 7).

Table 7 *Communicating by telephone*

Disadvantages
- Possible lack of rapport
- Forming erroneous impressions of the other person
- Easy to get distracted
- Temptation to do two things at once
- Low social presence
- Lack of non-verbal cues
- Lack of documentary support
- More difficult to detect deception than face to face

Advantages
- Quick, easy and cheap means of communication
- Easy to get in touch with busy people
- Easier to be assertive and authoritative
- Saves time
- Can facilitate bargaining and persuasion

In many cases it is easier to get in touch with someone by telephone than in person. People usually answer the telephone and are less likely to begrudge the time spent on a phone call than in a meeting for which they have to travel.

It is also possible to take advantage of the way that people form impressions on the phone. For example, you are more likely to be able to be assertive and authoritative on the telephone, and since the other person cannot see you, you are free to assume any personality you choose. Also, many people find it easier to be firm on the phone, perhaps because they are not distracted or intimidated by the reactions of the other person.

Telephone conversations tend to be shorter than face-to-face conversations, so the phone can save time in this way too, and reduce the time spent in travelling or letter writing.

Interestingly, research shows that it can be easier to change someone else's beliefs over the telephone than face to face. This also holds true for bargaining and negotiation, when it seems that the side with the stronger case is more likely to win when discussing the problem over the phone than when discussing it face to face.

Overall, the telephone as a medium is more formal than face-to-face communication, less spontaneous and more depersonalised. This formality can act to your advantage if you want to win an argument or put over a certain impression of yourself. Remember that since the non-verbal aspects of the interaction are virtually nil, you may need to compensate for this by using a warm tone of voice and lots of responses, like 'yes' or 'uh-huh', while the other person is talking, to show that you are listening.

checklist of good telephone behaviour

- Try to answer the telephone promptly and always give your name and position.
- If you are calling someone else, ask if it is a convenient time to talk. If not, establish a time at which you will call again, and stick to it.
- If you receive a call at an inconvenient time, say so and proceed as above.
- Always say, early on, why you are calling; don't leave your partner wondering what is going on.
- Use the other person's name to increase friendliness.
- Listen carefully to the other person and take notes of the call.
- Summarise your own contribution from time to time to ensure that the other person clearly understands what you are saying.
- Try not to be distracted by events around you.
- When you are concluding a call, go back over what you have agreed and re-state any action that needs to be carried out.
- Always try to end on a friendly note to take advantage of the 'recency' effect.

GROUP DISCUSSION

Form into groups of three or four people. Each group should consider how a school-leaver who is going to spend most of the day dealing with clients on the telephone might be trained. Make a list of the important skills that he or she has to master.

---

teleconferencing

There are many ways in which to hold meetings at a distance, either via a system which links voice only or via one which also supplies a picture of the participants. This section begins with a brief review of some of the systems available.

group telephone systems

These are often known as conference calls. Each person sits at a telephone and the switchboard operator links up participants so that they can all talk to each other. One system typically accommodates about eight people at once. However, sound quality can be less than satisfactory and the main problem is how to control the interactions.

Loudspeaking telephones can also be included under this category, e.g. DORIC from British Telecom. Here participants as a group are seated around a loudspeaker. This is connected to a loudspeaker at the other end with another group of people around it. As each person speaks, that contribution is sent to the other group's loudspeaker. However, it can be hard to distinguish individual speakers, unless they say who they are every time they speak.

Finally there is the Remote Meeting Table which is used mainly by the British Civil Service. Here, two groups of up to six people sit around a table. Each person has a microphone which is linked to a loudspeaker at the other end. When a person speaks, his or her voice comes through one particular loudspeaker on which that person's name is shown and which lights up to indicate who is talking.

videotelephones

Here speakers are linked not only by telephone but also have an optional video of each other. This system was designed to allow visual cues to be transmitted. It has not been a successful medium to date, probably because it is very expensive.

A similar system – British Telecom's Confravision – links up studios in several cities in the UK. Participants sit in a studio and can see the people in the other studio(s) on a black-and-white television monitor. There are two cameras, one for documents and the other to show the participants, and two television screens, one showing each group. There are several systems of this type now available throughout the world.

the effects of different media

So what effects does the medium of communication have? The first area concerns person perception. Often meetings are the first opportunity for business contacts to get to know one another. The main area of interest here is that of confidence. It has been found that people are more confident in their judgement of another person if they can see as well as hear the other person, although in most cases their judgements do not change according to the medium of communication. This can be important in a work context, especially if the participants do not know each other. It may be that it is more difficult to make confident estimates of colleagues if a mediated communication system is being used.

People tend to prefer systems which incorporate visual communication as well as just sound. However, a study by Tomey (1975) found that there were advantages to the sound-only system. He looked at an audio-only conferencing system used for bank committee meetings. The participants saw the meetings as more impersonal than face-to-face meetings but this was compensated for by certain advantages:

- Overall discussion of specific items tended to be shorter.
- It was easier to get over a point without a lot of debate.
- The members of the committee were more attentive.

This indicates that electronic meetings may be more business-like in the way they are run.

Overall, electronic meetings are suitable when the meeting is to be task-oriented and indeed may be better than face-to-face meetings for this purpose. However, when person-oriented tasks are to be fulfilled, then a face-to-face approach is best.

Table 8 *The main advantages and disadvantages of using a teleconferencing system*

Advantages
- Teleconferencing promotes greater meeting efficiency and faster decision-making, and therefore leads to shorter meetings. It is especially useful for emergency meetings where the participants are geographically distant.
- Teleconferencing can be useful to decentralised companies with distributed workforces that need to work closely on projects. It allows for closer work cooperation.
- It increases the range of communication opportunities (e.g. when bad weather prevents travel).
- Travel time can be saved, thus allowing busy people to meet.
- Being part of such a system can increase personal status.
- It can lead to increased supervision and reporting by personnel.
- It can increase cooperation and coordination.

Disadvantages
- Decreased social presence of participants.
- Participants may need to learn new skills to operate the system and to run meetings effectively.
- Expensive to implement.
- There can be user resistance to the new medium and uncertainty over whether the system is effective.
- Not suitable for 'getting to know people' situations or for general assessment of others.

communicating by computer

As computers and communications networks become more common, new communications choices are becoming possible, including computer conferencing, electronic mail and voice messaging. Whilst these provide people and organisations with more choice of communications systems and services, it also means we need to understand how to make the best use of this choice of communication medium, so as to choose the most appropriate channel and make the communication most effective.

computer conferencing

This is the most recent development in conferencing. PLANET was the first one offered commercially (by Infomedia in California). Each person has a computer terminal into which he or she can type information. All the terminals are linked up to a central computer. There are usually two ways of holding the conference: synchronous and asynchronous. In *synchronous conferencing* all the participants are actually seated at their terminals at the same time and can type in questions and comments, send documents, etc. These are sent by the computer to all participants. It is also possible to send private messages to particular people. *Asynchronous conferences* are much the same but are often extended over weeks or months. These systems are now popular and common amongst groups of scientists and some branches of government.

Computer conferences, particularly the ongoing asynchronous conferences, have a number of potential benefits. Firstly, they provide an easy way of broadcasting views and information to a fairly large number of people in a number of different locations. This is particularly the case when there is difficulty in reaching a number of people in a short time, as larger groups of people on more sites can simultaneously receive a single transmission of information that can normally only be accommodated with audio or video conferencing.

Asynchronous conferences allow local meetings and interruptions to take place and the ongoing conference to be picked up later, when convenient, since all the exchanges are available in rejoining the conference.

Computer conferencing is particularly useful to facilitate coordination and information sharing and it encourages lateral communication. However, because it is a text-based medium, computer conferencing tends to be less interpersonal and more 'formal' than face-to-face, video or audio conferencing. It has a low level of social presence.

Another drawback to this medium is that with a wide potential audience there can be a tendency to make extreme statements on positions rather than comments that directly address another person.

Finally, where there is a conflict to resolve between extreme positions, it may be necessary to get on the telephone to sort it out, or even hold a face-to-face meeting.

electronic mail

Electronic mail is a computer-based postal service. Electronic mail differs from computer conferencing as messages are sent only to those directly addressed rather than to all the participants in a conference. It can be used, however, to broadcast a message to everybody within an organisation. More typically, large organisations in government, commerce and academia provide electronic mail networks to facilitate internal and external person-to-person communication.

Although electronic mail is typically used for short and frequently informally phrased text messages, some electronic mail systems also transmit documents.

The principal benefit of electronic mail is that it is a quick way of sending a text message across continents and time zones. We can leave a note in another person's mailbox. However, unlike the telephone it is not so easy to know whether or not the person at the other end has received or read the message. One of the problems is to persuade people who use the system actually to read their messages.

Perhaps one of the reasons for this is that it is so quick and easy to send a message, and often easier to send a message to everybody than to a selected few, people can end up getting a lot of messages. Unlike the letter post, where a glance at the envelope often gives an idea of the contents, it is necessary to open and read each electronic letter before knowing that it can safely be ignored.

Both computer conferencing and electronic mail systems need a widespread acceptance if they are to be an effective means of communication.

voice messaging

Voice messaging works in much the same way as electronic mail except that it is a voice recording that is stored in the mailbox rather than electronic text.

Voice messaging systems range from the home telephone answering machine, through centralised voice mailboxes, to communicating computer sytems that allow voice 'notes' to be attached to documents. Voice messaging has the advantage of asynchrony without having to be near a computer since the service can be accessed by telephone. Voice messages tend to be seen as less formal than electronic mail messages and are used in less formal ways. Voice recordings also differ from text as they are difficult to scan and edit and cannot be printed out.

Short, informal messages are the best way of using voice messaging. It is useful to make notes both before using such a system and when listening to one.

recommendations on the use of electronic mail and voice messaging

- Use your electronic mail service regularly. Try to read your mail every day and respond promptly to messages.
- Use text-based services for more formal messages, and voice mail or annotation for the less formal messages.
- Think about the reader of your message. A well-structured message using a good format will be seen as more professional.
- Title your message clearly.
- Consider who is receiving your messages – choose your address list carefully. Who really wants or needs your message?

PRACTICAL EXERCISE

Form into pairs. Design a presentation for your group which covers the technological media available and the advantages and disadvantages of each one.

suggestions for further reading

Bretz, R. (1983) *Media for Interactive Communication*, Sage, California. Good survey of some modern communications media.

Christie, B. (ed.) (1985) *Human Factors of Information Technology in the Office*, John Wiley and Sons Ltd, London. Not a light read, this book covers the psychology of using and designing information technology in the office.

Short, J., Williams, E. and **Christie, B.** (1976) *The Social Psychology of Telecommunications*, John Wiley and Sons, London. A useful overview of what the different media are good for.

glossary

attribution theory   A social psychological theory that examines how people decide on the causes of their own behaviour, or the behaviour of others.

behaviourist theories   A group of psychological theories that concentrate on the study of behaviour without considering any cognitive or motivational aspects.

black box approach   Another term for behaviourist theories such as Skinner's.

classical conditioning   A type of learning through the association of stimulus and response, first put forward by Pavlov.

epistemic freezing   The point at which cognitive / mental activity is frozen / stopped and no further information is sought.

figure and ground   A concept put forward by Gestalt psychologists which says that we separate things into shapes or figures set against a background.

fundamental attribution error   We tend to ascribe the causes of behaviour to people's personality rather than to the situation they are in.

groupthink   A term coined by Janis who argued that group norms develop which will boost group morale at the expense of clear, logical thinking. It causes the group to stop seeking information. Likely to occur when the group is highly cohesive and closely knit, and faces a difficult/threatening situation.

Hawthorne effect   By merely studying behaviour at work, performance is improved.

heuristic   A mental rule of thumb from which we arrive at answers by means of a limited information search.

ingroup   The group to which a person feels that he or she belongs and can identify with.

managerial grid Conceived by Blake and Mouton, a grid onto which managers are placed and evaluated for the degree of orientation to people and task.

non-verbal communication Communication which does not involve language.

OB Mod *O*rganisational *B*ehaviour *Mod*ification focuses on how rewards and punishments can shape people's behaviour.

operant conditioning The idea that learning is based on getting rewards.

outgroup A social group to which one does not belong nor identify with.

path goal theory Subordinates' behaviour can be influenced by rewards. Paths to these rewards must be easily understood, and rewards are contingent on behaviour.

primacy The tendency to give too much credence to early-encountered information.

principle of closure We tend to fill in gaps, often unconsciously.

principle of proximity We tend to group things together if they are physically near each other.

principle of similarity We tend to group things together if they are similar.

psychometric tests Tests which are used to measure psychological characteristics, e.g. intelligence, creativity, personality.

social facilitation A phenomenon whereby the presence of others enhances individual performance of simple tasks.

social loafing A tendency in group members to 'take it easy', since they believe their inaction will be masked by the activity of others.

stereotype A generalisation about an individual or group (often unjustified).

Trait theory A theory of personality which involves comparing people on the basis of certain aspects of behaviour, or traits, which are believed to be stable and enduring.

valence The anticipated satisfaction or dissatisfaction associated with an outcome.

Vroom and Yetton model A leadership model which depends on the decision-making ability of the leader.

useful references

Abercrombie, K. (1968) 'Paralanguage', *British Journal of Diseases of Communication* **3**, 55–59.

Alderfer, C. P. (1972) *Existence, Relatedness and Growth*, Free Press, New York.

Alberti, R. and **Emmons, M.** (1975) *Stand Up, Speak Out, Talk Back: The key to assertive behaviour*, Impact, San Luis Obispo, California.

Allen, T. J. and **Marquis, D. G.** (1964) 'Positive and negative biasing sets: the effects of prior experience on research performance', *IEE Transactions and Engineering Management* **EM-11,** 158–61.

Argyle, M. (1975) *Bodily Communication*, Methuen, London.
(1988) *The Psychology of Interpersonal Behaviour*, Penguin Books, Harmondsworth.

Argyle, M. (ed.) (1981) *Social Skills and Work*, Methuen, London.

Argyle, M. and **Cook, M.** (1976) *Gaze and Mutual Gaze*, Cambridge University Press, Cambridge.

Argyle, M. and **Ingham, R.** (1972) 'Gaze, mutual gaze and distance', *Semiotica* **6**, 32–49.

Aronson, E., Willerman, B. and **Floyd, J.** (1966) 'The effect of a pratfall on increasing interpersonal attractiveness', *Psychonomic Science* **4,** 157–58.

Asch, S. E. (1946) 'Forming impressions of personality', *Journal of Abnormal and Social Psychology* **41,** 258–90.

Atkinson, G. M. (1975) *The Effective Negotiator*, Quest, London.

Beattie, G. (1981) 'A further investigation of the cognitive interference hypothesis of gaze patterns during conversation', *British Journal of Social Psychology* **20,** 243–48.

Belbin, R. M. (1981) *Management Teams*, Heinemann Educational Books, London.

Bergen, H.B. (1939) 'Finding out what employees are thinking', *The Conference Board Management Record*, April 1939.

Berkowitz, L. (1986) *A Survey of Social Psychology*, CBS Publishing Japan Ltd.

Biddle, D. and **Evenden, R.** (1980) *Human Aspects of Management*, Institute of Personnel Management.

Blake, R. R. and **Mouton, J. S.** (1978) *The New Managerial Grid*, Gulf Publishing Co., Houston, Texas.

Blum, M. L. and **Naylor, J. C.** (1968) *Industrial Psychology: Its theoretical and social foundations*, Harper and Row, New York.

Brown, H. (1985) *People, Groups and Society*, Open University Press, Milton Keynes.

Bugelski, B. R. (1973) *An Introduction to the Principles of Psychology*, Babbs-Merrill Co. Inc.

Carnegie, D. (1971) *How to Win Friends and Influence People*, Chaucer Press, Bungay, Suffolk.

Chell, E. (1987) *The Psychology of Behaviour in Organizations*, Macmillan, London.

Cohen, C. E. (1981) 'Person categories and social perception: testing some boundaries of prior knowledge', *Journal of Personality and Social Psychology* **40**, 441–52.

Christie, B. (ed.) (1985) *Human Factors of Information Technology in the Office*, John Wiley and Sons Ltd, London.

Debus, G. and **Schroiff, H. W.** (eds.) (1986) *The Psychology of Work and Organization*, Elsevier Science Publishers BV, Holland.

Deutsch, M. (1949) 'A theory of cooperation and competition', *Human Relations* **2**, 199–232.

Dion, K. K., Berscheid, E. and **Walster, E.** (1972) 'What is beautiful is good', *Journal of Personality and Social Psychology* **24**, 285–90.

Druckman, D. (ed.) *Negotiations: Social psychological perspectives*, Sage, Beverly Hills.

Duncan, S. and **Fiske, D. W.** (1977) *Face-to-face interaction: Research, methods and theory*, Lawrence Erlbaum Associates, Hillsdale, New Jersey.

Dyer, W. G. (1984) *Strategies for Managing Change*, Addison-Wesley, Redding, Mass.

Eiser, J. R. (1980) *Cognitive Social Psychology*, McGraw-Hill, Maidenhead, Berks.

Ekman, P. and **Friesen, W. V.** (1967) 'Head and body cues in the judgement of emotion: a reformulation', *Perceptual and Motor Skills* **24**, 711–24.

Evans, D. W. (1986) *People, Communication and Organisations*, Pitman Publishing, London.

Feldman, D. C. and **Arnold, H. J.** (1983) *Managing Individual and Group Behaviour in Organizations*, McGraw-Hill Inc., Tokyo.

Fiedler, F. E. (1967) *A Theory of Leadership Effectiveness*, McGraw-Hill, New York.

Fisher, J., Rytting, M. and **Heslin, R.** (1975) 'Hands touching hands: affective and evaluative effects of interpersonal touch', *Sociometry* **39**, 416–21.

Furnham, A. (1979) 'Assertiveness in three cultures: multidimensionality and cultural differences', *Journal of Clinical Psychology* **35**, 522–27.

Giles, H. and **Powesland, P. F.** (1975) *Speech Style and Social Evaluation*, Academic Press, London.

Hall, E. T. (1966) *The Hidden Dimension*, Doubleday, New York.

Hall, C. S. (1954) *A Primer of Freudian Psychology*, New American Library.

Hammond, L. K. and **Goldman, M.** (1961) 'Competition and noncompetition and its relationship to individual and group productivity', *Sociometry* **24**, 46–60.

Hargie, O. (1986) *A Handbook of Communication Skills*, Croom Helm, London/New York University Press, New York.

Hargie, O., Saunders, C. and **Dickson, D.** (1987) *Social Skills in Interpersonal Communication*, Croom Helm.

Henley, N. M. (1977) *Body Politics*, Prentice-Hall, Englewood Cliffs, NJ.

Honey, P. (1988) *Improve Your People Skills*, Institute of Personnel Management.

Hunt, J. (1981) *Managing People at Work*, Pan Books Ltd, London.

Janis, I. L. (1972) *Victims of Groupthink: A psychological study of foreign-policy decisions and fiascoes*, Houghton-Mifflin, Boston.

Jones, W. H., Hobbs, S. A. and **Hochenburg, D.** (1982) 'Loneliness and social skill deficits', *Journal of Personality and Social Psychology* **42**, 682–89.

Kendon, A. (1967) 'Some functions of gaze direction in social interaction', *Acta Psychologica* **26**, 22–63.

Kogan, N. and **Wallach, M. A.** (1964) *Risk-taking: A study in cognition and personality*, Holt, New York.

Lange, A. and **Jakubowski, P.** (1976) *Responsible Assertive Behaviour*, Research Press, Champaign, Illinois.

Lawler, E. E. (1973) *Motivation in Work Organizations*, Brooks/Cole, Monterey, California.

Lawler, E. E. III (1977) 'Reward systems' in J. R. Hackman and J. L. Shuttle (eds) *Improving Life at Work*, Scott, Foresman & Co., Glenview, Illinois.

Lett, R. E., Clark, W. and **Altman, I.** (1969) *A Propositional Inventory of Research on Interpersonal Space*, Washington: Naval Medical Research Institute, Washington.

Lewin, K., Lippitt, R. and **White, R. K.** (1939) 'Patterns of aggressive behaviour in experimentally created social climates', *Journal of Social Psychology* 10, 271–99.

Lieberman, S. (1956) 'The effects of changes in roles in the attitudes of role occupants', *Human Relations* 9, 385–402.

Lowin, A. and **Craig, J. R.** (1968) 'The influence of level of performance on managerial style. An experimental object lesson in the ambiguity of correlational date', *Organizational Behaviour and Human Performance* 3, 440–58.

Lott, A. J. and **Lott, B. E.** (1968) 'A learning theory approach to interpersonal attitudes' in A. G. Greenwald, T. C. Brock and T. McOstrom (eds) *Psychological Foundations of Attitudes*, Academic Press, New York.

Lott, D. F. and **Sommer, R.** (1967) 'Seating arrangements and status', *Journal of Personality and Social Psychology* 7, 90–95.

McClelland, D. C. (1961) *The Achieving Society*, Van Nostrand, Princeton.

Maslow, A. H. (1954) *Motivation and Personality*, Harper, New York.

Miller, G. A. (1977) *Psychology. The science of mental life*, Pelican, London.

Morley, I. E. (1981) 'Bargaining and negotiation' in C. L. Cooper and P. Makin (eds) *Psychology for Managers*, BPS and Macmillan, London.

Moscovici, S., Mugny, G. and **Van Avermaet** (eds) (1985) *Perspectives on Minority Influence*, Cambridge University Press, Cambridge.

Nadler and **Lawler** (1977) 'Motivation and Diagnostic Appraisal' in E. Hackman (ed) *Perspectives on Behaviour in Organisations*, McGraw-Hill, New York.

Newman, H. (1982) 'The sounds of silence in communicative encounters', *Communication Quarterly* 30, 142–49.

Rackham, N. and **Carlisle, J.** (1978) 'The effective negotiator – part I', *Journal of European Industrial Training* 2, 6–10.

Reddin, W. J. (1970) *Managerial Effectiveness*, McGraw-Hill (UK) Ltd, London.

Rotter, J. B. (1966) 'Generalized expectancies for internal versus external control of reinforcement', *Psychological Monographs* 80, 1, Whole No. 609.

Salancik, G. R. and **Pfeffer, J. A.** (1978) 'A social information processing approach to job attitudes and task design', *Administrative Science Quarterly* 23, 224–53.

Scherer, K. (1979) 'Acoustic concomitants of emotional dimensions: judging affect from synthesised tone sequences', in S. Weitz (ed.) *Nonverbal Communication: Readings with commentary*, 2nd ed, Oxford University Press, New York.

Scott, W. (1986) *The Skills of Communicating*, Gower Publishing, Hampshire.

Sherif, M. (ed.) (1962) *Intergroup Relations and Leadership*, Wiley, New York.

Short, J., Williams, E. and **Christie, B.** (1976) *The Social Psychology of Telecommunications*, John Wiley and Sons, London.

Siegel, J. (1980) 'Effects of objective evidence of expertness, nonverbal behaviour and subject sex on client-perceived expertness', *Journal of Counselling Psychology* **27**, 117–21.

Sidney, E., Brown, M. and **Argyle, M.** (1973) *Skills With People. A guide for managers*, Hutchinson & Co., London.

Skinner, B. F. (1953) *Science and Human Behaviour*, Macmillan, New York.

Stogdill, R. M. (1948) 'Personal factors associated with leadership: a survey of the literature', *Journal of Psychology* **25**, 35–71.

Stogdill, R. M. (1974) *Handbook of Leadership: A survey of theory and research*, New York Free Press, New York.

Tiffin, J. and **McCormick, E. J.** (1970) *Industrial Psychology*, Unwin University Books, London.

Taylor, D. S. and **Wright, P. L.** (1988) *Developing Interpersonal Skills*, Prentice Hall International.

Tomey, J. F. (1975) 'The field trial of audio conferencing with the Union Trust Company', Unpublished report from the New Rural Society Project, Fairfield University, Connecticut. Cited in **Christie, B.** (1985).

Tysoe, M. (1988) *All This and Work Too. The psychology of office life*, Fontana, London.

Vroom, V. H. (1964) *Work and Motivation*, Wiley, New York.

Vroom, V. H. and **Jago, A. G.** (1978) 'On the validity of the Vroom–Yetton model', *Journal of Applied Psychology* **63**, 151–62.

Vroom, V. H. and **Yetton, P. N.** (1973) *Leadership and Decision Making*, University of Pittsburgh Press, Pittsburgh.

Walster, E. (1965) 'The effects of self-esteem on romantic liking', *Journal of Experimental Social Psychology* **1**, 184–97.

Warr, P. B. (ed.) (1978) *Psychology at work*, Penguin, Harmondsworth.

Wilson, G. and **Nias, D.** (1976) *Love's Mysteries: The psychology of sexual attraction*, Open Books, London.

appendix

How to determine your managerial style

Choosing the elements that fit you best

Consider all of the '1' element statements below (**A1**, **B1**, **C1**, **D1** and **E1**) and circle the one that best describes your behaviour. Follow the same procedure for the '2', '3', '4', '5' and '6' elements.

Element 1: Decisions

A1 I accept the decisions of others with indifference.
B1 I support decisions that promote good relations.
C1 I search for workable, even though not perfect, decisions.
D1 I expect decisions I make to be treated as final.
E1 I place high value on sound, creative decisions that result in understanding and agreement.

Element 2: Convictions

A2 I avoid taking sides by not revealing opinions, attitudes and ideas.
B2 I embrace opinions, attitudes and ideas of others rather than push my own.
C2 When others hold ideas, opinions or attitudes that are different from my own, I try to meet them half way.
D2 I stand up for my ideas, opinions and attitudes, even though it sometimes results in stepping on toes.
E2 I listen for and seek out ideas, opinions and attitudes that are different from my own. I have strong convictions, but respond to sounder ideas than my own by changing my mind.

Element 3: Conflict

A3 When conflict arises, I try to remain neutral.

B3 I avoid generating conflict; but, when it does appear, I try to soothe feelings to keep people together.

C3 When conflict arises, I try to find fair solutions that accommodate others.

D3 When conflict arises, I try to cut it off or win my position.

E3 When conflict arises, I try to identify reasons for it and seek to resolve underlying causes.

Element 4: Temper

A4 By remaining uninvolved I rarely get stirred up.

B4 Because of the disapproval tensions can produce, I react in a warm and friendly way.

C4 Under tension I feel unsure and anxious about how to meet others' expectations.

D4 When things are not going right, I defend, resist, and come back with counter-arguments.

E4 When aroused, I contain myself even though my impatience is visible.

Element 5: Humour

A5 My humour is seen as rather pointless.

B5 My humour shifts attention away from the serious side.

C5 My humour sells me or my position.

D5 My humour is hard-hitting.

E5 My humour fits the situation and gives perspective; I retain a sense of humour even under pressure.

Element 6: Effort

A6 I put out enough to get by.

B6 I prefer to support others rather than initiate action.

C6 I seek to maintain a steady pace.

D6 I drive myself and others.

E6 I exert vigorous efforts and others join in.

Open and candid communication is the link between people that permits sound problem-solving and decision-making. Without them an organisation is unlikely to succeed. With them it is able to maximise its use of human resources. The grid concentrates on what makes person-to-person communication ineffective, what makes it effective, and what to do to change ineffective into effective communication.

Determining *your* managerial style

You may find it valuable to assess communications in your own managerial behaviour. Rank the paragraphs that follow from *most typical* to *least typical* as a description of your behaviour; 5 is most typical, 4 is next most typical, and so on to 1, which is least typical. When you have finished ranking the paragraphs, there should be only one of each number from 5 to 1. There can be no ties. Before starting, a word of caution: self-deception is likely to occur when you pick your answers. The deception is caused by the tendency of people to confuse the way they *want* to manage with the way they *do* manage.

The first step in accurate self-assessment is to strip away self-deception in order to see your underlying assumptions. Some self-deception is probably unavoidable, although it can be reduced by selecting answers based on your *actual* performance as a manager. This is a starting-point for improving your managerial effectiveness.

A I accept the decisions of others with indifference. I avoid taking sides by not revealing opinions, attitudes and ideas. When conflict arises, I try to remain neutral. By remaining uninvolved I rarely get stirred up. My humour is seen as pointless. I put out enough to get by.

B I support decisions that promote good relations. I embrace opinions, attitudes and ideas of others rather than push my own. I avoid generating conflict; but, when it does appear, I try to soothe feelings to keep people together. Because of the disapproval tensions can produce, I react in a warm and friendly way. My humour shifts attention away from the serious side. I prefer to support others rather than initiate action.

C I search for workable, even though not perfect, decisions. When others hold ideas, opinions or attitudes that are different from my own, I try to meet them half way. When conflict arises, I try to find fair solutions that accommodate others. Under tension I feel unsure and anxious about how to meet others' expectations. My humour sells me or my position. I seek to maintain a steady pace.

D I expect decisions I make to be treated as final. I stand up for my ideas, opinions and attitudes, even though it sometimes results in stepping on toes. When conflict arises, I try to cut it off or win my position. When things are not going right, I defend, resist and come back with counter-arguments. My humour is hard-hitting. I drive myself and others.

E   I place high value on sound, creative decisions that result in understanding and agreement. I listen for and seek out ideas, opinions and attitudes that are different from my own. I have strong convictions, but respond to sounder ideas than my own by changing my mind. When conflict arises, I try to identify reasons for it and seek to resolve underlying causes. When aroused, I contain myself even though my impatience is visible. My humour fits the situation and gives perspective; I retain a sense of humour even under pressure. I exert vigorous effort and others join in.

Now, copy the table below and transfer your initial rankings to the two left columns (under 'Initial'). The first column is for 'Paragraphs', the second is for 'Elements'.

The first paragraph, A, is called the 1,1 paragraph. It is followed, in order, by B–1,9, C–5,5, D–9,1 and E–9,9. The same order applies for each element. The first phrase under 'Decisions' (A1) describes the 1,1 attitude. It is followed by B1–1,9, C1–5.5, D1–9,1, and E1–9,9. The same order applies for each of the other elements.

Now it is possible to interpret your selection of grid styles to depict your own managerial behaviour.

Assessment of my grid styles

Initial		
Paragraphs	**Elements**	
A(1,1) ____	1 Decisions ____	____
B(1,9) ____	2 Convictions ____	____
C(5,5) ____	3 Conflict ____	____
D(9,1) ____	4 Temper ____	____
E(9,9) ____	5 Humour ____	____
	6 Effort ____	____

Did you come out as predominantly 9,9? Or was it 9,1, 1,9, 1,1 or 5,5? If what you saw was 9,9, is that the 'real' you? Is your approach really from a 9,9 direction, or is it possible that you have misread yourself? We know that self-deception is common.